WHISPERS OF MERCY

A Poetic View of God's Grace
in the Story of Jonah

Lewis C Alexander

What's Write For Me, LLC

CONTENTS

LEWIS C ALEXANDER

SUMMARY

Whispers of Mercy: A Poetic View of God's Grace in the Story of Jonah

Embark on a contemplative journey through the biblical account of Jonah, reimagined through poignant poetry. This lyrical exploration invites readers to slow down, breathe deeply, and embrace God's tender mercy. Through powerful verse, author Lewis C Alexander guides readers into the heart of Jonah's story —from fleeing God's presence to embracing His tender mercy. Each poem whispers truths about God's gracious nature, His slow anger, and His relentless love. Whispers of Mercy inspires reflection:

Will we surrender to God's mercy or flee from His call? How will Jonah's story unfold in our lives?

Join the journey. Let poetry become prayer. May God's gentle voice remain within your heart—guiding you homeward with grace upon grace.

DEDICATION

To my beloved mother Mary Bess, whose love reflected God's grace – and to all who wander in darkness, searching for solace. May these whispers of mercy guide you home to God's loving embrace.

FOREWORD

As you breathe in these whispers of mercy, may poetry become prayer, guiding you deeper into the Scripture's embrace. These pages invite your soul to slow its pace, breathe deeply, and linger in contemplation, meditating on the themes of God's grace woven throughout Jonah's story and these poetic reflections.

As mercy whispers truths to your heart, may you embrace the Scripture's wisdom and poetry's gentle nudges, transforming mere words into spiritual nourishment for your journey.

INTRODUCTION

B efore the belly of the beast, there was a whisper.

This collection began not as a book, but as a prayer—formed in the quiet spaces of grief, longing, and rediscovery. Jonah's story has long echoed in my own: a calling heard early, a season of fleeing, and a return shaped by mercy. These poems are not just retellings of Scripture; they are reflections of a soul learning to listen again.

Each verse is paired with a personal reflection, an offering of testimony, a glimpse into the journey that led me back to the light I once fled. My hope is that as you read, you'll find your own story woven between the lines. That Jonah's descent and return will mirror your own moments of wrestling, surrender, and grace.

We begin in the depths, with a prayer rising from the belly of brokenness. Out of the Beast is not just Jonah's cry—it was mine. And perhaps, it has been yours too.

JONAH 2:1

Then Jonah prayed unto the Lord his God out of the fish's belly.

OUT OF THE BEAST

In darkest depths, I cried to Thee,
A prayer that rose from misery.

The world's loud lies had sought to claim my heart, drown my soul in shame.

But you, O Lord, heard my plea,

And from the waves, You lifted me.

Rescued me from the beast's dark night and guided me into your living light.

The lies that bound me, you broke them clean, set me free. In your presence, is liberty.

I'll rise, O Lord, and walk with Thee,

And in your love, I will be free.

LA

REFLECTION: OUT OF THE BEAST

There was a time I believed that I could outrun the calling placed on my life. My first poem was published in the third grade—a whisper of purpose I didn't yet understand. As I grew older, life's storms gathered. My parents divorced and I became bitter, angry and ashamed. I thought I had caused the fracture and in that pain, I turned away from God. I hid my face and ran to the world, searching for solace in places that only deepened the ache.

For years I fled, like Jonah—thinking I could discard the divine invitation. Grief has a way of calling us home. After losing my father, then more than two decades later, my mother. I found myself broken. In the quiet aftermath, I turned to writing, not as an escape, but as a way to process the sorrow. In those sacred moments of reflection. I rediscovered the home I had left so long ago.

God met me in the depths. His mercy lifted me from the belly of grief and guided me back into his light. What I thought was the end became a beginning. The calling I had once fled, became the very path of healing.

JONAH 1:3

But Jonah rose up to flee unto Tarshish from the presence of the Lord, and went down to Joppa; and he found a ship going to Tarshish: so he paid the fare thereof, and went down into it, to go with them unto Tarshish from the presence of the Lord.

FLEEING HIS LIGHT

Jonah ran, God's voice denied,
A ship to Tarshish, mind astride, heart searching for a place to hide.

Storms surged, guilt's heavy weight,

Fleeing God seals mortal fate.

Yet mercy waits, though depths consume—

Grace revives in ocean's tomb.

LA

REFLECTION: FLEEING HIS LIGHT

Before I ever cried out from the depths, I chose to flee. Like Jonah boarding the ship to Tarshish, I paid the fare to escape the presence of God—not with coins, but with years of bitterness, shame and self-imposed exile. I believed the lie that I was disqualified, that my brokenness had voided the calling placed on me as a child. That early poem, published in the third grade, became a distant echo. One I tried to silence beneath the noise of the world.

I ran hard. I buried my gifts beneath grief and distraction, convincing myself that God's light was too pure for someone like me. Even in my rebellion, mercy waited. Storms came, not to punish, but to awaken. Loss stripped away my defenses. The passing of my father, then later my mother, became sacred turning points. In grief, I stopped running. In silence, I heard His whisper again.

Fleeing His Light reminds me that God's presence is not something to fear. It is the very place where healing begins. The ship I boarded to escape, became the vessel that carried me back to grace. I write, not to hide, but to illuminate. Not to flee, but to follow.

JONAH 4:2

And he prayed unto the Lord, and said, I pray thee, O Lord, was not this my saying, when I was yet in my country? Therefore, I fled before unto Tarshish: for I knew that thou art a gracious God, and merciful, slow to anger, and of great kindness, and repentest thee of the evil.

TENDER MERCY

You are gracious, slow to wrath,
In love, You pave a tender path.
Compassion flows, unfailing, free,
A God who loves relentlessly.
Your mercy reigns eternally.
LA

REFLECTION: TENDER MERCY

When I finally stopped running, I didn't find judgement. I found tenderness. I had braced myself for rebuke, expecting God to echo the shame I had carried for so long. He whispered mercy instead. Like Jonah, I knew deep down that God is gracious, slow to anger and his mercy is never ending. This truth has always lived in me, even when I tried to suppress it.

In the quiet of grief, I began to write again. Not just to process pain, but to rediscover purpose. Each word became a prayer, each poem a step in the journey of healing. I saw that God had never abandoned me. He had waited patiently, though not always gently, guiding me back to him. His mercy was not a one-time rescue. It was a daily invitation to walk in his grace.

Tender Mercy reminds me that God's kindness is not a weakness. It is his strength, wrapped in compassion. It is the kind of love that doesn't force, but woos. It doesn't condemn, it restores. I fled because I believed that I was unworthy. Now I write because I know I am loved.

This journey, from the belly of grief to the light of grace. Isn't just Jonah's story. It's mine and perhaps yours too.

LEWIS C ALEXANDER

AFTERWORD

As whispers of mercy fade into silence, may God's gentle voice remain within your heart—guiding you homeward.

May the Scripture's truths and poetry's reflections merge into prayer, sustaining your spirit with grace upon grace.

Go slowly, breathe deeply, and lean into his embrace. May God's love accompany you always."

COMPLETING JONAH'S STORY: A PERSONAL JOURNEY

T he book of Jonah ends abruptly—no final redemption scene, no conclusive character arc. Intentional silence invites us to become Jonah. To flee or follow God's whisper, to resist or embrace mercy.

These poems inspire reflection:

The next few pages allow space to answer these questions for yourself.

How will Jonah's story
unfold in my life?

Write your answers, prayers or devotional questions below.

Will I surrender to tender mercy
or flee from God's call?

Write your answers, prayers or devotional questions below.

BENEDICTION

May you walk gently into the days ahead,

with mercy as your companion and grace as your guide.

When the call feels distant or the path unclear,

may you remember Jonah—and remember yourself.

That even in fleeing, God pursues.

Even in silence, He speaks.

Even in sorrow, He heals.

May the whispers of mercy linger in your soul,

reminding you that you are not forgotten,

not forsaken,

but forever invited.

May your gifts rise again,

your heart soften,

and your story unfold in the light of His love.

Amen

Go now—beloved, called, and held.

And when you hear His whisper,

may you have the courage to say yes.

Out of The Beast

Jonah 2:1
Then Jonah prayed unto the Lord his God out of the fish's belly.

In darkest depths, I cried to Thee, A prayer that rose from misery. The world's loud lies had sought to claim My heart, drown my soul in shame. But you, O Lord, heard my plea, And from the waves, You lifted me. Rescued me from the beast's dark night and guided me into your living light. The lies that bound me, you broke them clean, set me free. In your presence, was liberty. I'll rise, O Lord, and walk with Thee, And in your love, I will be free.

LA

11/28/24

Tender Mercy

Jonah 4:2
And he prayed unto the Lord, and
said, I pray thee, O Lord, was not
this my saying, when I was yet in
my country? Therefore I fled before
unto Tarshish. For I knew that thou
art a gracious God, and merciful,
slow to anger, and of great kindness,
and repentest thee of the evil.

You are gracious, slow to wrath,
In love, You pave a tender path.
Compassion flows, unfailing, free,
A God who loves relentlessly.
Your mercy reigns eternally.
LA

Fleeing His Light

Jonah 1:3
But Jonah rose up to flee unto Tarshish from the presence of the Lord, and went down to Joppa; and he found a ship going to Tarshish: so he paid the fare thereof, and went down into it, to go with them unto Tarshish from the presence of the Lord.

Jonah ran, God's voice denied.
A ship to Tarshish, mind astride, heart searching for a place to hide.

Storms surged, guilt's heavy weight,
Fleeing God, seals mortal fate.

Yet mercy waits, though depths consume
Grace revives in ocean's tomb.
LA

LEWIS C ALEXANDER

BOOKS BY THIS AUTHOR

The Grove Of Plenty: A Story Of Hope And Harvest

Discover the intersection of hope and kindness in "The Grove of Plenty" and "Vigilant Sight". This ebook and poem duo explores the human experience through the lens of compassion, empathy, and community. Join Ricardo and Rachel on a journey of transformation and growth, and be inspired to spread kindness and love in your own community.

Journal Of Faith: A 30-Day Devotional Built To Strengthen Your Faith

Embark on a transformative spiritual journey with this 30-day journal. Explore inspirational Bible verses, reflection prompts with space for prayer and gratitude. Deepen your faith, cultivate hope and experience God's love and guidance. The thought provoking prompts in this journal guide readers to delve deeper into each verse, exploring their personal significance and application in everyday life. By reflecting on these prompts, readers can uncover new insights, cultivating a richer understanding of God's word and develop a more intimate relationship with the creator.

Faith Unshaken: Trusting God Through Persecution

WHAT IF THE ANCIENT STORY OF DANIEL ISN'T JUST HISTORY

BUT A DIVINE ROADMAP FOR TODAY'S TRIALS?

In Faith Unshaken, discover how Daniel's unwavering trust in God amidst persecution mirrors the challenges believers face today. From fiery trials to modern marginalization, this powerful devotional shines a light on God's unchanging faithfulness. With scripture-based insights and timely encouragement, you'll find strength to stand firm when your faith is tested. Let this book inspire you to trust boldly, live courageously, and anchor your hope in the One who never fails.

Made in the USA
Middletown, DE
15 November 2025

21525260R00020

From Slavery to Freedom

Wishing you
all God's freedom —

Jeff

Other books in the Lutheran Voices series

From Slavery to Freedom
A Personal Reading of the Exodus Story

Jeffrey A. Krogstad

Augsburg Fortress

Minneapolis

FROM SLAVERY TO FREEDOM
A Personal Reading of the Exodus Story

Purchases of multiple copies of this book are available at a discount from the publisher. For more information, contact the sales department at Augsburg Fortress, Publishers, 1-800-328-4648, or write to: Sales Director, Augsburg Fortress, Publishers, Box 1209, Minneapolis, MN 55440-1209.

Materials for a single- or multiple-session study of *From Slavery to Freedom* are downloadable free of charge at www.augsburgfortress.org.

Library of Congress Cataloging-in-Publication Data

Krogstad, Jeffrey A., 1966–
  From slavery to freedom : a personal reading of the Exodus story / Jeffrey A. Krogstad.
    p. cm.
  Includes bibliographical references.
  ISBN 978-0-8066-5772-1
  1. Bible. O.T. Exodus I-XX—Criticism, interpretation, etc. 2. Liberty—Religious aspects—Christianity. I. Title.
  BS1245.52.K76 2009
  222'.1207—dc22
                              2009006709
The paper used in this publication meets the minimum requirements of American National Standard for Information Sciences—Permanence of Paper for Printed Library Materials, ANSI Z329.48-1984. Manufactured in the U.S.A.

Contents

Preface

For freedom Christ has set us free. Stand firm, therefore, and do not submit again to a yoke of slavery. (Gal. 5:1)

What does it mean to be "free in Christ"? What does this freedom look like? Is it available to *anyone*? How can we begin to experience it? If we follow Jesus, from what are we set free? And for what reason? If freedom is so near to the heart of the Christian message, why do so few Christians live "free"? This book is an attempt to answer these questions.

Many people have contributed, directly and indirectly, to this work. I can't begin to acknowledge all those who have taught me about Christian freedom. But a few specific thanks are in order: my thanks to Susan Johnson at Augsburg Fortress for her encouragement, support, and insight; to an amazing staff team at Central Lutheran Church in Elk River, Minnesota, with whom I am privileged to work; to the Alpha Leadership Team at Central, especially to those who read and offered feedback on early manuscripts; and to a diverse group of church leaders in the central Philippines who were the first to hear me teach on this material. To my wife Julie and our daughters Erica and Mathea: thank you for helping me experience freedom and for living into God's dreams with me!

My prayer as you read this book is that you will learn what it means to live free in a relationship with Jesus—that the same God who set the Israelites free from slavery sets you free as well. Whatever keeps you in slavery, whatever weighs you down, God is able to set you free. May you experience all the joy and all the fullness of life that God longs to give you!

Introduction

Finding Yourself in Chains

Bible Basis: Exodus 1

So the Egyptians made the Israelites their slaves. . . . (Exod. 1:11, NLT)

Melinda came to see me at the church office just a few days after she got out of treatment for alcohol abuse. She needed to talk about her experience and to share what was now clear to her. "Pastor, I was a slave to alcohol," she began. "I would leave my kids at home and go drink. I'd drink away the mortgage check. My husband and I would drink together until we both passed out." She paused briefly to collect herself. "I needed to know that I was a slave, but no one ever told me. Why didn't anyone ever tell me?"

Without a word, I pulled a hymnal off a bookshelf and turned to the liturgy we used every Sunday to confess our sin. I pointed to the words that Melinda, along with the rest of the congregation, had spoken in worship on countless occasions:

Most merciful God, we confess that we are in bondage to sin and cannot free ourselves. We have sinned against you in thought, word, and deed, by what we have done and by what we have left undone. We have not loved you with our whole heart; we have not loved our neighbors as ourselves. For the sake of your Son, Jesus Christ, have mercy on us. Forgive us, renew us, and lead us, so that

9

we may delight in your will and walk in your ways, to the glory of your holy name. Amen."[1]

Melinda's eyes grew large as she heard the familiar words as if for the first time. "This is it!" she almost shouted. "This is exactly what I needed to hear! Why couldn't I hear it before?"

When we are enslaved to sin, it's hard to hear the truth.

It is troubling how easily we give ourselves over to sin, how something quite innocent becomes an obsession. For instance, I have always loved horses. My older brother got a horse when I was seven, but by the time I was old enough to ride on my own, the novelty had worn off for my brother, and, to my dismay, my parents sold the horse. Whenever I mentioned my desire to get a horse of my own, their response was always, "We tried that."

Years later, a friend who owns horses invited me to ride whenever I wished. I eagerly accepted the invitation and spent many wonderful hours grooming, saddling, and riding my friend's horses, all the while yearning more and more to have a horse of my own. Then one day another friend offered me a horse for free. Imagine, a free horse!

My veterinarian cautioned me that a free horse isn't usually a bargain, but I saw the offer as my dream come true. I refused to be deterred by the fact that we live in a subdivision that doesn't allow livestock. And I figured out that if my wife worked a couple more days a month, we would have enough money to buy food, tack, and equipment and to cover veterinary bills.

It turned out that the "free" horse was dangerously overweight. Worse, she wanted nothing to do with me. When I finally managed to mount her, we had our own private rodeo. But none of that mattered to me. I desperately wanted a horse of my own, and I saw this as a chance to get what I wanted. My obsession with owning a horse—even an overweight, unruly one—ate up my leisure time, lowered my performance on my job, and put tension in my marriage.

Thankfully, I recognized the danger before permanent damage was done, but to this day, I am amazed by the seductiveness of what began as an innocent dream.

It's clear to me now that my obsession with owning a horse was part envy, part idolatry. In fact, my desire to own a horse ended up owning me. The Apostle Paul wrote about the power of sin to enslave not only our bodies but the whole of our being: "When you follow the desires of your sinful nature, the results are very clear: sexual immorality, impurity, lustful pleasures, idolatry, sorcery, hostility, quarreling, jealousy, outbursts of anger, selfish ambition, dissension, division, envy, drunkenness, wild parties, and other sins like these" (Gal. 5:19-22, NLT).

Some of the things Paul names are self-explanatory, both in terms of what they mean and how they can become destructive forces in our lives. But there are others on Paul's list that, without some explanation, we might too easily dismiss as having no hold on us. Let's take a closer look at a few of the behaviors Paul warns about.

"Impurity" is letting unclean thoughts, perspectives, and attitudes occupy our thoughts, words, and actions. It's what your mom may have called, "having your mind in the gutter."

"Idolatry" means worshiping other gods. No problem, right? Don't be so sure. On what do you spend your money? What takes up most of your time? What pushes God out of the way in your life? A car, a mortgage, a hobby, a job, even family can become an idol that pushes God out of the way and enslaves us.

At its root, "sorcery"—the practice of casting spells and manipulating unseen powers—is about a deep need to have control. Are you a control freak? Does the need to be in control of yourself and your environment affect your relationships with other people? What about your relationship with God? The desire for control can mess up our spiritual lives in a hurry, because this desire is directly opposed to letting God be in control.

"Jealousy" is the desire to possess a person. It is rooted in fear. I've met with many couples where the husband was so afraid that his wife would leave him that he tried to control her friendships, her outside activities, her job, and even her phone conversations. Deep down, such men don't believe they are worth sticking around for, and as a result they live with passionate jealousy disguised as love.

"Dissension" is caused by always disagreeing with others. No matter what someone says, you profess to hold the opposite viewpoint. You might say, "I just like to play devil's advocate." Think about that statement! There's nothing wrong with evaluating what someone says. That's healthy. But if you're always pushing your viewpoint and rarely supporting someone else's statements, beliefs, or ideas, you might be a slave to dissension.

"Division" is the desire to split a group. There are people who can't stand to see any organization united behind a common goal. Division is closely related to dissension, but it goes a step farther. Division takes the disagreement and builds a coalition that works against leadership to paralyze the organization. I knew a man once who made seventeen phone calls every Sunday afternoon. The first sixteen were to contact his "friends" and complain about the pastor's sermon. The seventeenth call was to the church council chairman to say, "People have been telling me they're pretty upset about the sermon this morning." This man was in bondage to division.

"Envy" has the potential for wreaking tremendous damage in our lives, not the least of which is that it poisons our ability to appreciate God's gifts to us. An envious person looks at another's life—what he owns, how he lives, who he's married to—and wants it . . . badly.

There are behaviors on Paul's list that fit a little too closely for comfort in my experience. It's hard to admit that sin clings so closely, but until we recognize that we live in slavery and can name that which binds us, we will never be free. The story of the Israelites'

exodus from slavery in Egypt to freedom in the Promised Land offers some important lessons in this regard.

Exodus tells how the Israelites were slaves in the land of Egypt and how God raised up Moses to set them free and lead them out of Egypt to the Promised Land. These events happened more than three thousand years ago, more than a thousand years before Jesus was born. Yet from that time down to today, the descendants of those Israelites remember the story of how God set them free. The Exodus story is key to Jewish identity—from ancient Israel to today. Down through the generations, the memory of the Exodus from slavery to freedom was kept alive. When Israelites, even hundreds of years later, brought their sacrifices to God, they would say, "*We* were slaves in the land of Egypt . . ." (see Deut. 6:20-21, emphasis added). The Exodus was not just a story of what happened back then; it was *their* story. And it is *our* story, too. For the God who through Moses rescued the Israelites from slavery in Egypt is the same God who through his Son rescues us from slavery to sin and sets us free. Like the ancient Israelites, we are called out of slavery to lives of blessing through the gracious act of a loving God.

For Reflection and Discussion

1. Look back at Paul's list of behaviors in the Galatians passage. With which do you identify?

2. Think of an example from your own experience when a desire became an obsession. How did you handle this?

3. Our worship liturgy includes the confession of sins. What comes to mind as you recite the words to the confession?

1

God Hears Our Cries

Bible Basis: Exodus 2–4

> God heard their groaning, and God remembered his covenant
> with Abraham, Isaac, and Jacob. God looked upon the Israelites,
> and God took notice of them. (Exod. 2:24-25)

Very near the beginning of the biblical book of Exodus is the
ominous announcement: "Now a new king arose over Egypt, who
did not know Joseph" (Exod. 1:8). Those dozen words foretell the
transformation of the Hebrew people from being welcome and
respected guests of one pharaoh to slaves of another. Think how
difficult such an abrupt change in status would be. What could the
Israelites do? I can imagine four responses:

1. Make the best of it: "Surely we can learn to find purpose and
   fulfillment in making bricks."
2. Attempt to negotiate better terms: "We will make your bricks,
   but we need time off from sundown Friday to sundown Saturday
   to keep the Sabbath."
3. Look for opportunities for advancement: "If we toe the company
   line, do an exceptional job, and don't make any trouble, we stand
   a good chance of being restored to our rightful place."
4. Live in the past: "Remember the good old days when Joseph—
   one of our own—was calling the shots?"

But the Israelites didn't choose any of these responses. The Bible indicates that it took the Israelites a while—at least the lifetime of one pharaoh—to fully grasp the reality of their enslavement. When they did, they *groaned* and *cried out* (see Exod. 2:23).

I understand groaning. It's a natural response in unbearable circumstances. Women in labor groan. Parents groan when unable to manage an unruly child. I witnessed a grieving husband groan and throw himself on his wife's coffin just before we lowered her into the ground.

But the Israelites did more than groan. They cried out, and not to just anyone, mind you; they cried out to God because they were wise enough (or desperate enough) to know that only God could help them. They cried out for God to remember the covenant God made with their ancestor Abraham. They cried out for God to remember them. They cried out for a miracle. They cried out to be saved.

As I said before, I understand groaning. In fact, I'm a good groaner. Sadly, I'm not as good about crying out. Too often when faced with adversity, my response has been to look for ways that *I* can make the situation better. I work harder and spend hours researching solutions. Or I seek diversions, and, if all else fails, I go on vacation.

Crying out to God means recognizing that I can't change the situation, but God can. Crying out means coming to the end of myself and admitting I need help. That's a lot to swallow for someone who takes pride in making it on my own (sinful as that may be). I suspect it's hard for you, too. In the end, crying out opens our lives for God's action. And have no doubt, God will act.

When the Israelites cried out, the first thing God did was raise up a leader named Moses. Let's take a look at Moses and see what we can learn about the kind of people God chooses to lead his people to freedom.

First of all, it's important to see what Moses was *not*. Moses was not qualified in any obvious way for the position to which God called him. He had no proven track record of leadership. What he did have was a bounty on his head for murdering an Egyptian overseer (see Exod. 2:11-15) and multiple excuses for why he wasn't the right person for the job (see Exod. 3:11—4:17).

Moses did bring some useful skills to the position, however. He knew the inner workings of Pharaoh's court because he grew up in Pharaoh's household after being saved as an infant by the king's daughter (Exod. 2:1-10). Moses also had experience in tending flocks (albeit animals, not people), and he knew something about wilderness navigation. Both were skills he acquired while herding sheep for his father-in-law Jethro. In fact, it was while tending Jethro's flocks that Moses acquired the single most important qualification for the job of leading the Israelites out of Egypt: on Mount Sinai, Moses met God (Exod. 3:1-6).

While there is a great deal of discussion about what it means to *do* the will of God, the Bible is absolutely clear about what God's will *is*. God's will is that all people be saved and come to know the truth (see 1 Tim. 2:4). God's agenda in freeing us from the power of sin is the same as God's agenda in freeing the Israelites from slavery: to bring us to himself. To this end God raises up leaders who know him—people whose own lives have been changed by meeting God—to help others meet him or come to know him better.

The words *transparency* and *authenticity* are mentioned a lot in leadership seminars as important attributes for effective spiritual leadership. Transparent, authentic leaders speak honestly about their encounters with God and how they have been changed through God's very real presence in their lives. They do not hide the sins God has forgiven them in the past nor deny that they continue to need God's forgiveness and healing today. But neither do they seek to draw attention to themselves by spilling their guts, weeping

openly, or confessing embarrassing sins publicly. Their words and actions bear witness to God's power—the power of love—to heal individuals and communities in a world broken by sin. Authentic spiritual leaders are servants.

What does it mean to be a servant leader? Google the term and you will find nearly 500,000 sites that discuss its meaning, from ministry to present-day business practices. Attributes of servant leaders include the ability to listen, empathize, bring healing and care, persuade, and build community. Servant leaders are humble and have foresight. They are able to put others ahead of themselves. If we think about the term in a biblical way, another name for *servant leader* might be *shepherd*, which brings us back to Moses.

God's appearance and call came as a big surprise to Moses. He didn't see himself as a great leader. He had settled quite nicely into a shepherd's life. But Moses recognized that he was standing in the presence of the Holy One, and despite his misgivings and excuses, he accepted the call to servanthood. God didn't send the rookie leader out empty-handed. He equipped Moses for the job. The staff Moses had used to herd the sheep and ward off predators became a tool to help lead the people out of bondage to freedom. It turned into a snake to show the people that Moses' power came from God (Exod. 4:1-5). It was used to bring plagues upon Egypt (Exod. 7:20; 8:16; 10:13). And when Pharaoh's army pursued them, Moses raised his staff and parted the waters so the people could escape (Exod. 14:16). Remember how the people groaned and cried out from bondage? They did in the desert too, and Moses struck the rock with his staff to get water (Num. 20:11). God hears the groans and cries of his people and acts by raising up leaders, big and small, to bring God's word of freedom and salvation.

Like Moses, we never know when or how God might use us. Like Moses, we may not see ourselves as leaders—servant or otherwise. We're more like the sheep—or the people—who needed to be led and rescued. So it's good that we have a Good Shepherd to

model a life of servant leadership for us and a God who equips us for the task by sending us the Holy Spirit (John 14:16-17, 26; Acts 1:6-8). We may not be called to lead a nation out of captivity—few people are. But we are called to serve in smaller ways: to help a friend who struggles in an unhappy marriage, to reach out to a grieving neighbor, to participate in civic activities that strengthen our communities and world. We are called to look beyond our groaning to hear the cries of others. And what we are able to accomplish is through God: "I can do all things through him who strengthens me" (Phil. 4:13).

For Reflection and Discussion

1. What situation in your life makes you groan?

2. Have you ever cried out to God and seen God answer? If so, what happened? Why is it so important that Moses has been to Mount Sinai?

3. How is God equipping you to be a servant leader?

2

Showdown with Power

Bible Basis: Exodus 5–7

But Pharaoh said, "Who is the LORD, that I should heed him and let Israel go? I do not know the LORD, and I will not let Israel go." (Exod. 5:2)

I wish that when Moses had told Pharaoh, "Let my people go," Pharaoh had responded, "Okay, if that's what God wants." But it didn't happen that way. And it doesn't happen that way in our lives either. The truth is, even though God has set us free through Christ Jesus, the powers that hold us captive fight tooth and claw to keep us in slavery.

Consider, for instance, alcohol addiction. Alcohol is chemical—a particular arrangement of carbon, hydrogen, and oxygen—and its effects on the human body can be fairly easily explained. But talk to recovering alcoholics, and they describe it quite differently. They say alcohol is a demon, a *spiritual* power. That's why in the Twelve Steps of Alcoholics Anonymous alcoholism is identified as a spiritual problem. Recovering alcoholics know they are fighting a spiritual battle.

Lutherans may not use "spiritual warfare" language as much as some other Christians, but we certainly recognize and reject the powers eager to keep us from experiencing the freedom God gives us. In fact, this is a very important part of our baptismal liturgy. Before pouring on the water, the pastor asks those of us assembled

to "profess your faith in Christ Jesus, reject sin, and confess the faith of the church."[1] What follows are three direct questions:

"Do you renounce the devil and all the forces that defy God?"

"Do you renounce the powers of this world that rebel against God?"

"Do you renounce the ways of sin that draw you from God?"

And the response to each of these is a resounding, "I renounce them." But it is only by God's grace that we can do this!

In the story of the Exodus, Pharaoh is the primary example of the powers that fight against God in order to keep us in slavery. When Pharaoh said he didn't know God, he wasn't saying he couldn't imagine or believe in God. Instead, he was saying he didn't recognize God as Lord, as Master, as Sovereign. Pharaoh wasn't ready to acknowledge that God was in charge. Pharaoh thought *he* was in charge, and he wasn't going to give up the Israelites without a fight. But God was prepared, and confident, in his choice of Moses to lead the people to freedom.

The God who sent Moses to rescue his people has a long history of patient watching, planning, and shepherding his people. Long before, when God chose the Israelites, he started with one man—Abraham—and made a huge promise to him: "I will make of you a great nation, and I will bless you, and make your name great, so that you will be a blessing. . . . and in you all the families of the earth shall be blessed" (Gen. 12:2-3). This promise came to Abraham and his wife Sarah when they were far too old to have children. In a miraculous way, God gave them a baby, Isaac, who was the child of the promise (see Gen. 21:1-3). And God's shepherding activity didn't stop with Isaac. God rescued Isaac's son Jacob from his brother Esau, from his uncle Laban, and from Jacob's own cheating schemes (see Genesis 27, 29, and 31). And God continued to act on behalf of God's people down through the generations. In fact, the story we're reading about Moses and the Israelites is just one step

in God's promise to bless the earth through Abraham's descendants. And don't miss this part: we are part of that same promise!

God remembered his promises to Abraham when he heard the groaning of the Israelites in Egypt. God remembers his covenant with us, too. When you cry out, God remembers that you are his beloved creation. He remembers what Jesus did for you at the cross. Jesus' death and resurrection is the fulfillment of God's promise to Abraham. God has not forgotten you. God has not forgotten his covenant promises. He will act.

But there are other powers at work, opposing God's plan. The summer I was eight years old, I accepted a motorcycle ride from an older neighbor kid. He took me down a remote road and raped me. Eight-year-old innocence suddenly gave way to hurt that I couldn't begin to understand. I learned from that experience never to be vulnerable. I learned to share only the surface of who I am and keep my true self hidden away. I learned that it's best not to talk about anything sexual, embarrassing, or painful. I learned that when I hurt, I'd better just deal with it myself—because no one else will help me. And all that "learning"—all those lies that I believed to be true—gave the powers that are opposed to God's love a place to work in my life.

Over the following decades, God fought a long battle against those powers. God broke down the fear, the pain, the shame and began—slowly, gently—to break through to an eight-year-old boy who needed to know the truth. He brought healing, a little bit at a time, to my wounded heart. God marshaled many resources to fight this battle in my life: a wife who loves me and holds me accountable, pastors who have spoken God's truth with love into my life, friends who refuse to be kept out on the edges of who I am, professional counselors, and the ongoing healing presence of his Spirit. I still live with old scars. But I have learned to share myself with others, to talk about difficult and embarrassing things, to let other people

help me when I hurt. Today I can tell you, freedom is a great and wonderful thing!

Just as God defeated Pharaoh and freed the Israelites, God frees us from the powers that want to keep their hold on us. That's God's promise to us made sure through the life, death, and resurrection of Jesus. That's God's promise to us received in baptism. By God's grace we are freed from the forces of evil and the power of sin. Hear the word that God spoke to the Israelites when the power struggle with Pharaoh started to heat up. Can you hear this as a word of promise to you as well?

> "I will take you as my own people, and I will be your God. You shall know that I am the LORD your God, who has freed you from the burdens of the Egyptians. I will bring you into the land that I swore to give to Abraham, Isaac, and Jacob; I will give it to you for a possession. I am the LORD." (Exod. 6:7-8)

Take a minute and imagine freedom. Imagine what it means for God to bring you "into the land"—into the promise, into the fullness of his love, his mercy, his grace. This is God's dream for you—this is what it means for him to be *your* God! Whatever those other powers are that want to keep you from God's promise, God is more powerful. He will not let anything keep you from his love.

For Reflection and Discussion

1. Have you known someone who has fought against alcohol or drug addiction into recovery? What was that journey like for that person?

2. What do you think it means when Lutherans say that the promised kingdom of God is "already, but not yet"? How are we living

in God's promises now? When will God's promises be finally fulfilled?

3. What is one area of your life where you have a hard time letting in God and/or other people? What might it mean for you to know God's love and power intimately in that area of your life?

3

Hardened Hearts

Bible Basis: Exodus 8–10

> But when Pharaoh saw that there was a respite, he hardened his
> heart, and would not listen to them, just as the LORD had said.
> (Exod. 8:15)

When I teach about the Exodus, by far the most common
question I'm asked is: How could God punish Pharaoh when it was
God who hardened Pharaoh's heart? It's not fair for God to harden
Pharaoh's heart and then torture all of Egypt and kill Pharaoh for
being hardhearted!

Fair is a dangerous word to use when we're talking about God.
Do we really want God to be "fair"? Do I want what I deserve from
God? No! Thank God that he is not fair! Thank God we don't get
what we have coming! In the end, this objection to how God acts
has more to do with mercy and less with fairness. We want—we
need—God to be merciful to Pharaoh, and to us. If God is not
merciful, we know we're sunk. If God hardens Pharaoh's heart and
then strikes him for being hardhearted, what is to prevent God from
treating us the same way?

Just what does it mean to be hardhearted? Other translations
of this text use "stubbornness" instead. I think we can all relate to
being stubborn at one time or another. We insist that our opinion is
the most important or we want things done our way, even when we

know our way is no better than another's. "It's my way or the high-way!" is the battle cry of the stubborn. When stubbornness becomes a habit and "hard" becomes the natural state of our hearts, then we have created a real problem for ourselves. Even though God is very good at breaking down our stubborn attitudes and getting through to us, God will let us shut him out of our hearts. It's as if God says, "Do you *really* want to live without me? Okay. Try it. I'll even help you."

This was Pharaoh's problem. Read through the whole story carefully and you'll find that while God said he would harden Pha-raoh's heart (Exod. 7:3), he doesn't *cause* it until late in the story. In the early part of the showdown, Pharaoh hardens his own heart. If you read chapter 8 of Exodus, you'll read twice that "Pharaoh hardened his heart" (Exod. 8:15, 32). Only after that does the story say explicitly that God hardened Pharaoh's heart (see Exod. 9:12; 10:20; 11:10).

But still—why would God do this? First of all, because God wanted to show Pharaoh who was in control:

> "For now I could have stretched out my hand and struck you and your people with pestilence, and you would have been cut off from the earth. But this is why I have let you live: to show you my power, and to make my name resound through all the earth. You are still exalting yourself against my people, and will not let them go." (Exod. 9:15-17)

God gave Pharaoh authority so that Pharaoh might proclaim God's greatness. But Pharaoh mistakenly believed he had power and he could do anything he wanted. God let Pharaoh harden his heart, just as God lets any of us harden our hearts if we choose. But as Pharaoh insisted again and again on hardening his heart, God took him a step farther. God hardened Pharaoh's heart even more, so that Pharaoh could experience his own sin, pride, and arrogance. It was

only then that Pharaoh began to experience the consequences of being hardhearted.

Because Pharaoh was king of the great land of Egypt, his hard heart had wide-ranging effects. God worked overtime on Pharaoh because God wanted to reach out to the land of Egypt. It wasn't just about Pharaoh as an individual—it was about his influence as well. Hear God's agenda for the Egyptians:

> "I will harden Pharaoh's heart, and I will multiply my signs and wonders in the land of Egypt. When Pharaoh does not listen to you, I will lay my hand upon Egypt and bring my people the Israelites, company by company, out of the land of Egypt by great acts of judgment. The Egyptians shall know that I am the LORD." (Exod. 7:3-5a)

God wanted the Egyptians to know him. God wasn't punishing the Egyptians; he was acting in love toward them. He wanted them—including their king—to know him! Yes, God's plan was to rescue the Israelites, but in such a way that the Egyptians got to witness divine power.

The first part of God's plan was that Pharaoh should know him;[1] second, that the Egyptians should know him. The third part of God's plan was to set the Israelites free in such a way that they would come to know him and to live as his people forever. From God's point of view, it's all about people living in a relationship with him!

Think about how God deals with us when we harden our hearts. God doesn't break us open by force, like cracking a walnut. God yearns for us to see that our prideful rebellion is killing us. God longs for us to long for him. If we choose to rebel, God will allow us to go our own way. If God calls us back again and again and we resist his loving call, he may change tactics and reinforce our arrogance until we get so sick of ourselves that we are finally broken, finally laid open to his plans, finally available for his work in our hearts.

A few years ago a mother asked me to help her son get off the streets and into a halfway house. Driving him to the house, I asked him point blank: "Are you playing the game to get a roof over your head, or are you really at a point where you want to change the way you live?" He smiled a knowing smile and said, "I'm pretty much playing the game. I wouldn't mind getting off drugs, but I don't want to have a job and pay rent. That's just not me."

This young man's heart was hard, and he was using anyone and anything he could find to keep from having to change. The best thing his mom could do was allow him to experience the consequences of his actions—poverty, homelessness, hunger, even illness if necessary—so he might begin to desire real change. As hard as it is to accept, if she truly loved him, she wouldn't help him.

Are there areas of your life that you want to change, but you're not willing to pay the cost? What would it take for you to want real change? Have you been guilty of hardening your heart when God has given you opportunities to change?

God's love is not a pie-in-the-sky sappy happy kind of love. God loves with a gritty, hard-edged love that will not settle for artificial smiles. God loves like a parent who is willing to do the hard part—even allow his child to suffer a little bit—in order to bring about lasting, loving change. God is crazy about you and won't let you go without a fight—even if the one he needs to fight is you!

For Reflection and Discussion

1. What is your reaction to God's hardening of Pharaoh's heart? Does it bother you? Why or why not?

2. Have you ever been hard-hearted? If so, what happened?

3. Have you ever seen a parent discipline a child by letting her experience the consequences of her choices? If so, do you think this is a loving thing for a parent to do? Why or why not?

4. In what areas of your life do you find yourself fighting against God most often? What would it mean to invite God to change you in those areas?

4

Foreshadowing Salvation

Bible Basis: Exodus 11–12

"For I will pass through the land of Egypt that night, and I will strike down every firstborn in the land of Egypt, both human beings and animals; on all the gods of Egypt I will execute judgments: I am the LORD. The blood shall be a sign for you on the houses where you live: when I see the blood, I will pass over you, and no plague shall destroy you when I strike the land of Egypt." (Exod. 12:12-13)

Nine times Moses went to Pharaoh and delivered God's message: "Let my people go." Nine times Pharaoh refused, and Egypt paid a terrible price: the Nile River turned to blood; frogs, gnats, and flies overtook the land; livestock sickened and died; boils festered on humans and animals; waves of hail destroyed property and lives; locusts invaded the land and ate every growing thing; for three long days Egypt was plunged into deep darkness. But, in the end, these demonstrations of power were just the prelude to what God would do to set his people free. When God's patience with Pharaoh ran out, he struck Egypt with the worst and final plague: the firstborn—human and animal—in every Egyptian household were killed. But the Israelites were spared.

God prepared the Israelites for that fateful night. Each household was instructed to slaughter a lamb and use a hyssop branch to

smear the lamb's blood around the doorway of their home. Houses marked with the blood of lambs were "passed over" when death visited Egypt, which is why we call that event *Passover*.

Imagine the Egyptians' grief when they discovered that "the firstborn of Pharaoh who sat on his throne to the firstborn of the prisoner who was in the dungeon, and all the firstborn of the livestock" had been killed (Exod. 12:29). Think of the shock when they learned that not a single Israelite had been harmed. No wonder Pharaoh summoned Moses while it was still dark and told him to go and to take the Israelites and the animals they tended with him. But it wasn't only Pharaoh who wanted the Israelites to get out of Egypt as fast as possible. The Egyptian people gave the Israelites precious jewelry and clothing and urged them to leave quickly. And they did. Without taking time to let the day's bread dough rise, the Israelites followed Moses out of the land where they had lived for over four hundred years. From that day forward, in the time of the first full moon of spring, the children of Abraham, Isaac, and Jacob share a ritual meal of roast lamb and unleavened bread to remember that God rescued them from slavery in the land of Egypt. It was this meal—the Passover Seder—that Jesus shared with his disciples on the night before he died. Jesus blessed the bread and wine and gave it to his disciples. "This is my body . . . this is my blood . . . take, eat in remembrance of me."

Traditionally, Christians have seen the events of the Passover as a framework for understanding what Jesus' death accomplished. There are some interesting parallels between these events, especially when considered around particular themes like authority, security, and pride.

Authority. Egypt was the strongest, wealthiest, and most advanced nation in the world at the time of the exodus. Since power and authority usually go hand in hand (might makes right), the Egyptians believed they had the right to enslave the Israelites. Nothing, not even God's show of power in the plagues, could

convince them otherwise. At least not until the tenth plague. The killing of the firstborn forced the Egyptians to recognize God's authority and bend to it.

Powers other than God claim to have authority over us, too. When we disobey God, Satan claims the right to invade our lives. But God's love and forgiveness, poured out in the death of his only son, destroyed Satan's power over us. Sin, death, and the power of the devil have no authority over those whom Jesus has "purchased and freed . . . not with gold or silver but with his holy, precious blood and with his innocent suffering and death."[1]

Security. The Egyptians believed that their wealth and military power would keep them safe. They were wrong about that—dead wrong. They learned the hard way that no army or worldly treasure could save their firstborn. But old illusions die hard. The Egyptians gave away their wealth to the Israelites as ransom for their own lives. And Pharaoh, who couldn't accept that mighty Egypt had been beaten by a bunch of slaves, lost his army to the Red Sea.

The powers of evil put their trust in deceit, manipulation, and fear. These are the tools Satan uses to enslave us. But Jesus robs Satan of his security by sending the Holy Spirit to create new life in us and fill us with the power and boldness of supernatural love. The powers of hell tremble in the presence of such love.

Pride. The armies of Egypt did not return victorious from the Red Sea. The Bible says the Israelites saw bodies of Egyptian soldiers lining the shore (see Exodus 14). Those who made it back to Egypt weren't greeted by cheering crowds but by more death, destruction, and disgrace. A mighty nation had been brought to its knees.

Centuries later another nation rose up to rule the ancient world. The Roman Empire was richer and more powerful than Egypt had ever been, and it liked to flex its muscles with public displays of its power. Conquered armies were paraded through the streets of Rome in something aptly called *triumphs.* These were glorious occasions. The victorious Roman army, led by the conquering general riding

in a grand chariot, marched through the streets amid the cheering crowds. In stark contrast, the conquered king—disheveled, disgraced, and wearing chains—walked with his defeated army. They were a public spectacle, greeted with laughter and scorn.

The New Testament describes what Jesus did at the cross like this: "He disarmed the rulers and authorities and made a public example of them, *triumphing* over them in it" (Col. 2:15, emphasis added). Jesus stripped Satan of his pride and exposed him for the liar and cheat he is. The powers of evil have been conquered. Jesus has plundered the treasures of hell and set us free.

There are certainly parallels between the Passover event and Jesus' death on the cross, but there is also an important difference. The difference has to do with *how* God saved us from the powers of sin, death, and the devil. God didn't triumph through might. God triumphed through love. Jesus was humble and obedient unto death.

The work needed to set us free is done. It was accomplished on the cross. Do you remember Jesus' last words? He said, "It is finished." Those weren't words of defeat. They were an affirmation of victory. God's work is done. Complete. Final. Never to be undone. The challenge for us is to learn to live in the freedom Jesus won for us.

For Reflection and Discussion

1. In what ways are we enslaved to a misplaced sense of authority, security, and pride?

2. Did you experience a different way of viewing the cross in this chapter? If so, what was different about it?

3. What is one area of freedom that is growing in your life as you work through this book? What is one roadblock you still struggle with?

5

Joseph's Bones

Bible Basis: Exodus 13

And Moses took with him the bones of Joseph who had required a solemn oath of the Israelites, saying, "God will surely take notice of you, and then you must carry my bones with you from here." (Exod. 13:19)

When the Israelites fled from the land of Egypt, they took along some strange baggage. They took with them the bones of Joseph, the young Israelite who generations before had risen to prominence in the pharaoh's court. They carried Joseph's bones with them to honor his dying wish. Weird, right? Not if you understand that Joseph recognized the truth: his people didn't belong in Egypt.

Maybe Joseph suspected that even though the Israelites were treated like royalty during his lifetime, someday that would change. More likely, Joseph remembered that God had made a covenant with his great-grandfather Abraham—the promise of land, nation, and blessing—and Joseph knew that one day God would fulfill his promise to bring them into their own land. When that happened, Joseph wanted to be in on it—if only to have his old bones reburied in the Promised Land.

So the Israelites fled the land with Joseph's old bones tucked in with the rest of their baggage. Imagine the memories those bones evoked for them. Not memories of the "good old days" when Joseph

was Pharaoh's right-hand man; those days had ended long before these Israelites were born. No, the bones evoked memories of years of forced labor, of being tired to the bone. Wrapped up in the sight of those old bones were years of pent-up feelings—humiliation, betrayal, anger, fear, hate—and painful memories of a past that the Israelites would have liked to forget.

We all have memories that we would just as soon forget. We all have skeletons in our closets—old bones that we work hard to keep hidden because the sight of them is so painful, secrets that we don't want exposed to the world. In my early thirties, I spent some time in counseling, dealing with the leftover baggage from being raped when I was a child. What I gradually—and painfully—came to understand was that that old skeleton in my closet was crippling my relationships with people I loved and who loved me. The path to healing included cracking open the closet door and shedding light on the secret inside. So I set about having quiet one-on-one conversations with my brothers and sisters, not knowing if they even knew what had happened to me as a child. Talk about terrifying— but what a gift those conversations turned out to be! In the course of sharing my story, I became privy to their stories. I learned about the bones they had carried for years. Working together to bring these painful memories to light reduced their stranglehold on all our lives.

My conversations with my siblings pried open the closet door part way, but because of what I learned from them, I realized that I needed to talk with my father as well. By then Dad was in his late seventies, and I wasn't sure if I had the courage to ask him to remember back to that terrible time so many years before. Would he be willing to talk with me about what had happened? Was I prepared to hear what he might say? These questions swirled around in my head as I drove home for a weekend with Dad.

I learned many things during a difficult conversation with my father that weekend. I learned about my father's efforts after my

assault to keep me and the other kids in the neighborhood safe in the future. I learned that contrary to what I had thought at the time—and all the years since—my hurt had mattered to my father. As he poured out his anger and his anguish about what had happened, I understood just how deeply it had mattered. In bringing into the open the pain I thought I had carried alone all those years, I learned just how much my father loved me. In a very real, yet quiet way, knowing this made all the difference in the world. Did it eliminate the pain? No, but it changed how I hurt. That weekend shed a little more light on those old bones I had hidden away for so many years.

Still, I needed to have one more conversation—this one with God. A few years passed before that conversation took place, but when it did, it lasted for hours. Little by little, as I confronted the lies and worked through the hurt, I came to see clearly that I had been living in slavery to fear and shame because of what had happened to me when I was a child. God gave me a vision of myself as small village surrounded by a solid wall that was both thick and high. There were gates in the wall that I passed through to work in the fields outside the wall and to interact with others. I saw that I looked happy when I was outside the walls, but my happiness ended when I retreated back behind the walls and isolated myself from others.

Then God showed me what he wanted to do in my life. God cut the walls apart, section by section, but I felt no fear watching this happen. I understood somehow that God wasn't punishing me by removing the walls. Instead, God's mercy and love for me was setting me free from the walls that kept me isolated rather than safe. God stacked the sections of wall in the field, building them layer upon layer until he had created a platform fifteen or twenty feet high. Then he led me up onto the platform and told me to look around. Even now I remember being amazed at how far I could see. I felt so free!

God isn't content to leave our pasts in the past, to let us stay in our hurt forever. God wants to free us from the mistakes, the regrets, the hurts, the shame, and the failures of our pasts so we can live fully today. Healing is a process, and it takes time. But as God patiently coaxes us away from the pasts that bind us, he equips us to live in the freedom he brings and to use what we have learned to help others find freedom. As the Apostle Paul told the Corinthians, God "consoles us in all our affliction, so that we may be able to console those who are in any affliction" (2 Cor. 1:4). God desires a future for you and for me that isn't rooted in our pain but in his goodness. God is good, and the Bible assures us that God works for good in all things (see Rom. 8:28). Some theologians talk about this as God redeeming suffering. I don't understand how this happens, but I've been on the receiving end of God working for good in my life often enough to know that it's true. Whether in past tribulations or future trials, God is with us. God is working hard to tear down the walls that keep us from knowing how much he loves us—enough to send his Son to die for us. God is working hard to pry open the closet doors that we use to keep out those who threaten to get too close to us—even those who love us.

So what are the skeletons in your closet, the hidden bones of your past that you don't want exposed to the world? What are the old hurts that you work so hard to keep hidden—often without even realizing it? God broke open places in my heart that I had kept tightly locked for decades. You can bet that God wants to bring healing and freedom to you, too.

For Reflection and Discussion

1. Spend some time journaling about your past—about the hurts and about the bright spots. How do you think God might want to use those events to shape your future? Remember as you write that God gave you your past for a reason!

2. If journaling is not your style, consider having a conversation with someone you trust, someone who knows Jesus. Tell that person your stories and share how you think God might be working through your past to create a new future. Before you begin, explain that this is not about rehashing old hurts; rather, you're trying to see your past the way God sees it.

6

God's Big Picture

Bible Basis: Exodus 14

> As Pharaoh drew near, the Israelites looked back, and there were the Egyptians advancing on them. In great fear the Israelites cried out to the LORD. (Exod. 14:10)

Talk about being caught between a rock and a hard place! With Pharaoh's army in hot pursuit behind them and the Red Sea stretched out before them, it looked like the great rescue would end almost before getting started. The Israelites thought so. They started crying for help, but soon their cries turned to accusations: "What have you done, Moses, bringing us out here to die? Didn't we tell you back in Egypt to leave us alone and let us serve the Egyptians?" (See Exodus 14:11-12.)

Really, shouldn't Moses have realized that Pharaoh might change his mind and come after the Israelites? Pharaoh had reneged before on agreeing to let them go. So wouldn't it have made sense to take a more direct route, say the fast road along the Mediterranean, rather than the roundabout way through the wilderness?

But God wasn't simply interested in getting his people away from Egypt. God's plan was to save them, to shape them, to make them his own—to renew with them the covenant he made with Abraham so that through them the whole of creation would be blessed. Caught, as they were, between a rock and a hard place, the

Israelites failed to see God's big picture. And Pharaoh, captured by his own sense of power, mistakenly thought that the Israelites' wilderness wandering was aimless—which was just as God had intended. In that moment when the Israelites faced near certain death and Pharaoh saw a chance to avenge the deaths of countless Egyptians, God determined that life would prevail. This moment would be branded onto their hearts. There would be no doubt about who had rescued them.

All this was lost on the terrified Israelites, raising a ruckus on the bank of the Red Sea, screaming for Moses to do something. But Moses understood that the next move belonged to God. Amazing as it may seem, Moses didn't know what God was going to do. He didn't have a clue as to what kind of plan God had for getting them out of this mess or what strategy God would employ. But Moses knew God. So when God said, "[L]ift up your staff, and stretch your hand over the sea and divide it, that the Israelites may go into the sea on dry ground," Moses didn't quibble with the plan, strange as it sounded (Exod. 14:16). Moses did what God said. He trusted in God's *faithfulness* rather than God's plan.

Moses lifted his staff and the waters parted and everything was sweetness and light, right? Probably not. The parting of the sea may have quieted the Israelites' fear of certain death rushing down on them with Pharaoh's chariots, but it likely created a whole new kind of fear. Imagine the Israelites looking at the path along the seabed with the walls of roiling water on either side and wondering how long it would stay that way, wondering if the waters would remain parted long enough for them to cross. Do you suppose the Israelites would have gone through the divided sea if Pharaoh hadn't been in hot pursuit? Doubtful. Fear drove them forward when Moses told them to walk into the Red Sea.

The fact is that enslaved people are fearful people, and fear is a powerful tool for keeping people enslaved. On that day God didn't free the Israelites from slavery to everything that bound them, but

the Red Sea crossing was one step in God's plan to do just that. God didn't free them from fear, but he freed them to face a particular fear and, in the process, to discover that God could be trusted.

We, too, are called to trust in God's faithfulness and unfailing love for us, but fear drives us to ask for plans and strategies. Fear keeps us from seeing God's big picture and makes us settle for knowing what to do in particular circumstances. We think we need to know the plan, when what we really need is to wait for God and to trust that God has our best interests in mind.

How often do we envision freedom to be far less than what God has in mind? For example, we set our sights on getting free from debt, while God is intent on making us generous stewards of the gifts he gives. Or husband and wife hope for relief from marital tensions, while God's design is that they come to cherish one another so deeply that others are blessed by the relationship they share. Or we pray for physical healing, while God desires us to be whole in body, mind, and spirit.

We have a vision for what we think freedom should be, but it doesn't come close to the vision God has for us. The danger is that we sometimes confuse our vision for God's. Within our limited vision of freedom, the responsibilities of daily living can become confining. Work can become a duty rather than a calling through which we can enrich the lives of others. Community life can become an obligation rather than a way to care for our neighbors. Even family can become a burden.

For busy people involved in the mundane tasks of daily living, with demands on our energy, time, and resources pulling us every which way, there's tremendous temptation to settle for a limited vision of freedom. When, like the Israelites, we find ourselves caught between a rock and a hard place, our inclination is to dive in and start swimming. But such hasty action carries the risk of drowning. Better that we wait for God. Remember what happened when Moses and the Israelites stood on the bank of the Red Sea and waited for

God? God honored their waiting by opening up a road through the waters—a way to escape Pharaoh's army and near-certain death by drowning. Exodus means "the road out." On that day God opened up a road out from slavery. God created a road to freedom.

God doesn't promise that by surrendering our visions to his we will get what we *want*, but like the Israelites, we will get what we *need*. Surrendering our visions opens up the way for God to work in our lives, not to free us from our responsibilities, but to help us see them in a new light. God is with us all the days of our lives, seeking every opportunity—even the hard moments of waiting—to make us his own. If we learn anything from the Red Sea event, it is that we shouldn't ask to see God's plan for our lives. We should ask to see *God*. Rather than ask for information about what's going to happen next, we should wait for God. We should trust in God's faithfulness.

Forty years after the Red Sea crossing, God called the Israelites to step into the swollen waters of the Jordan River and wade across to the land he had promised them. The journey to freedom involved passing through the water, trusting that God would be with them on the other side as he had been with them every day of the journey.

For Reflection and Discussion

1. How would the Israelites' story be different if Pharaoh had simply let the people go? How does the experience of going through the Red Sea change the story?

2. Are there areas of your life where you feel like you are caught between Pharaoh's army and the Red Sea? How does it feel just to wait in that place?

3. What is the difference between trusting God's plan and trusting God? Why is it dangerous to put our trust in God's plan?

4. What are the human obligations and covenants that tie you down? How might God use these ties to make you even more effective in his kingdom?

7

We're Free! Or Are We?

Bible Basis: Exodus 15

"The LORD is my strength and my might,
    and he has become my salvation;
this is my God, and I will praise him,
    my father's God, and I will exalt him.
The LORD is a warrior;
    the LORD is his name.
"Pharaoh's chariots and his army he cast into the sea;
    his picked officers were sunk in the Red Sea." (Exod. 15:2-4)

Can you imagine the excitement the Israelites felt as they climbed out of the seabed, even with Pharaoh's army in hot pursuit? As the last of the Israelites worked their way up the bank, God acted yet again and the sea closed over the armies of Egypt. In a moment of stunned silence, the Israelites must have asked themselves, Can it be true?

At that moment, even when there were still questions to ask and problems to solve, the Israelites showed that this miracle was God's victory, not theirs. Led by Moses and his sister Miriam, the Israelites took time to celebrate on the banks of the Red Sea. In fact, they wrote a song to remember this victory!

When God sets you free, when you see him win a victory in your life—small or large—it is important to pause and praise. That's what

worship is all about. When we thank God, sing to him, rejoice in what he has done, and tell the stories of his victory, we accomplish at least three things. First, we remind ourselves that this is God's victory, not ours. Second, we tell the people around us that God is good, that he is trustworthy, that his love and his mercy will come through for us. Third, we make space in ourselves for stronger faith. As we praise God for what he has done, we learn to trust him for what he will do.

Praising God in solitude is good. But this kind of party is so much better in a group! People who say they don't need the church are missing out on this kind of communal celebration. When we gather together and tell stories about what God has done, we reinforce each other's faith. We build each other's trust. We grow each other's strength. This is one reason why most worship services include reading the Bible aloud. The psalmist declares, "Let them extol him in the congregation of the people, / and praise him in the assembly of elders" (Ps. 107:32), and "Ascribe to the LORD the glory due his name; bring an offering, and come into his courts" (Ps. 96:8), and again, "I will tell of your name to my brothers and sisters; / in the midst of the congregation I will praise you" (Ps. 22:22). Many Bible readings tell stories of what God has done in the past. Peter's sermon to the throng at Pentecost in Acts 2 and the role call of the faithful in Hebrews 11 are prime examples of God's past activity that assure us that God will be at work in our lives today!

Another dimension of this celebration includes recording what God has done for us so we don't forget. When God acts in our lives in a very real way, when we experience God's goodness concretely, it's easy to think we'll always remember. But encounters with God can be like mountaintop experiences. You think the memory will never fade, but a year or two later, you may have trouble remembering details of the depth of God's goodness. Write this story down! Even if it's intensely personal and you don't think you'll ever share

the details with anyone, write it down and put it someplace private. Then go back from time to time and remember the way God has worked to set you free!

Remember that from beginning to end, this is a story of what it means to live in relationship with God—the God who sets us free, the God who leads us toward the Promised Land. While our freedom was gained once and for all in the death and resurrection of Christ, our daily walk of faith is often one of starts and stops, of detours and wandering. Like the Israelites who came out of the Red Sea only to face the desert ahead, we face our own kind of wilderness. We may question why everything does not go just the way we want it in our lives. Perhaps we struggle with illness or depression or a difficult work environment or an estranged family relationship. Sometimes the journey from slavery to freedom feels just too long. Will we ever reach the Promised Land?

Tentatively, slowly, the Israelites began to push on into the wilderness. They had no consistent source of food or water. When they came to a spring, they dove in—only to find that the water was too bitter to drink. What a disappointment! They named the place "Bitter" (*Marah*) because of the water (see Exod. 15:22-25).

In the Bible, water is often a symbol of God's Spirit (see John 7:37-39, for example), and in the waters of baptism we are filled with that Spirit. The Spirit living in us becomes an internal guide, a wise teacher, and a source of strength for God's people: "Out of the believer's heart shall flow rivers of living water" (John 7:38).

But when the Israelites came to the water, it was bitter, and only through God's intervention was the bitterness removed. God showed Moses a piece of wood, and Moses threw it into the water. Through this strange act, God made the bitter water sweet. What can we learn from this? The hardest teachings of God's Spirit—like submitting our wills to God's will—can only be swallowed with the help of God. Just as God provided Moses with a piece of wood to take away the bitterness, we have been given the cross of Christ to

remove the bitterness of our sin. The cross is central to our journey of faith.

Let's say you're struggling with materialism. Your desire for things drives a wedge between you and God. The call to place God ahead of all your desires seems like a bitter burden. But God's Spirit calls you back to the cross. You remember that Jesus gave up everything to become human and to die for you. As you focus on the cross, the toys that seemed so important lose their shine. Submission to God's Spirit becomes not a trial you have to endure but a way to grow into the example of Jesus. If we want God to make use of our lives, there will be times when his Spirit needs to lead us into hard places, wilderness places. There may be bitter truths to swallow. If we don't keep the cross at the center of the truth, we may reject the ways God wants to help us grow.

Remember, God's agenda is not just to set us free. God wants us to grow close to him. At Marah, God instructed the people to "listen carefully to the voice of the LORD your God ... and give heed to his commandments," but his tone was gentle: "I am the LORD who heals you" (Exod. 15:26). What assurance! Whether our hurts come from old slavery to sin or the Spirit of God stretching us, God wants to be "the LORD who heals."

Exodus 15 begins in praise and ends in a place of promise—a foretaste of the feast that is to come. The Israelites moved on to a place called Elim, an oasis in the Sinai desert with twelve springs and seventy palm trees. Elim was a resting place, but not the final destination. It was a place of plenty, a place of fullness, a place of promise. They were free from slavery now, but God didn't want to simply set them free *from* something. He also wanted to set them—and us—free *for* something!

On your journey through the wilderness, God will sometimes bring you to a place of rest. It will be refreshing, full of his Spirit. You will enjoy the chance simply to relax in the good gifts of God. Take a deep breath. Learn what God has placed in front of you there

to learn. Thank God for the rest. But don't build a house. You're not in the Promised Land yet. You may have been freed from slavery, but God is calling you into a fuller, deeper freedom.

For Reflection and Discussion

1. Take a few moments and think of one thing God has done in your past that showed his power in your life. If you're with others, tell that story. If you're alone, spend a few minutes praising God for his goodness, his power, and his love for you. Try reading Moses' song in Exodus 15 aloud as a way to praise God!

2. What is one area in your life in which you think God might want to bring healing—physical, emotional, spiritual?

3. When was the last time you were at "Elim"—a place of rest and refreshment in spiritual terms? What was it like? How might you structure a time of rest and refreshment into your spiritual life in the next month?

8

Into the Wilderness

Bible Basis: Exodus 16

> The whole congregation of the Israelites set out from Elim; and
> Israel came to the wilderness of Sin. (Exod. 16:1a)

We live most of our lives in the wilderness. At the risk of spoiling the end of this book, you will not make it fully into the Promised Land this side of heaven. But life with God in the wilderness can be very, very good. And if we do not learn to live with him *now*, I can't imagine we'll experience much joy living with him *then*! Living in the wilderness shaped the Israelites to live in daily dependence on God. He had proved to his people that he could provide them with water. But what about food? Once again, the people began to grumble, yearning for the oversize meat kettles and vegetable gardens of Egypt. They were afraid of starving to death—and can you blame them?

Once again, God heard their cries and provided for them, sending a strange kind of food that settled with the dew on the surface of the ground. The people didn't know what it was, but they gathered it each morning. The word *manna* actually means, "What is it?" in Hebrew. Every time they said the name, the people were reminded of the mystery in this food, and in God's providing.

What does it mean to live in the wilderness? When God sets us free from bondage, we enter a whole new kind of life. In some

ways it's exciting to live without the old limits, the old slavery. But in other ways it's frightening. For example, maybe you're free from compulsive outbursts of anger, but now you have to deal with vulnerability in your relationships. You may have walked through the Red Sea away from a habit of impure thinking, but now you need to learn to define boundaries in your thought life and your conversations with coworkers. The hard reality is that in the past, our slavery gave life structure. When we're set free from that bondage, we face the dizzying problem of learning to live with uncertainty and with many choices.

What are some of the hard lessons we learn in the wilderness?

1. Give up control. Our plans are at the mercy of the weather, the trails, and a host of other variables. A couple years ago our family took a week-long canoe trip to the Boundary Waters in northern Minnesota. I picked out a lake that looked great on the map and planned the trip: one hard day to paddle in, several days exploring from base camp, and a hard day to paddle out. But what looked good on paper didn't pan out in reality. From day one our plans went right out the window. A portage that on our map looked fairly short and easy turned out to be steep and rocky and took much longer than we had planned. The whole day turned out to be much harder than we expected. We ended up cutting our plans short and setting up our base camp only a few miles from our entry point. Our plans had to change—we were not in control.

As we learn to trust God each day, we must learn to hold our plans loosely. Our desire to control our schedules and our agendas flies directly in the face of living in dependence on God.

2. Value portability. When the Israelites came out of Egypt, they immediately had to adapt to a nomadic lifestyle. They lived in tents. Later, when they built a worship center, they built it with portability in mind. You can't very well move a stone temple from place to

place—so God directed them to build a "tabernacle," a tent where they could meet with God.

We live in a portable world. The other day I got an e-mail from a friend who lives in Hawaii, telling me about an online seminar taking place in California. In a matter of minutes, sitting in my office in Minnesota, I had accessed the seminar's Web site and heard an excellent presentation. I then shot off an e-mail to my friend in Hawaii thanking him for the link.

Believers today need a portable faith. We need to carry it with us, just as we carry our Blackberries. A portable faith helps us carry God's message wherever we go. It means that God can work as hard in our offices, our classrooms, or our businesses as he does in our churches. It means that our homes can become gathering places for believers, not just our churches. Maybe God wants to use you not in a Bible study but in a seemingly random conversation at the grocery store. How will we reach people who don't know God's love if we're stuck in our bricks-and-mortar churches? We must be portable to live as God's people in the twenty-first century.

3. Value relationships. During a bear hunt one October, my younger brother Darin and our oldest brother Kevin were putting up a tree stand. We were miles from the nearest paved road, an hour from the nearest hospital. I was on the ground beneath the tree while Darin and Kevin were perched twelve feet up, adjusting straps and tightening bolts. As Kevin started down the tree, he slipped and fell ten feet, landing on his head and one shoulder. I was sure he was dead, until he began to groan. Darin ran through the woods to get his truck while I prayed and tended to Kevin. Had he been alone, it would have been nine or ten hours before anyone came looking—who knows what would have happened? As it was, he broke both arms and three ribs, but miraculously not his neck.

Life today is dangerous. Between crazy schedules, broken relationships, economic pressures, and spiritual malnutrition, people fall

hard every day. Relationships are critical for survival in the wilderness. We need each other. It is incredibly foolish to try to live alone in the wilderness of the twenty-first century.

4. Trust your navigator. Many cars today come equipped with a GPS navigation device that can direct the driver where he or she wants to go. The systems are not without their glitches, but by and large they are quite helpful! We have something like a GPS—only better—to guide us on our journey of faith. We have the Holy Spirit, our counselor and guide, and we have the Holy Scriptures, God's Word. It's important to know how to discern what God's Spirit is doing here and now. A friend of mine in her fifities has discovered a deep love for the Bible. She is constantly evaluating her life based on what she learns from God's Word. We can take a lesson from her! Daily Bible reading and prayer help keep us in close connection with the Spirit. Asking for guidance and trusting that the Spirit will lead us, we can navigate through the landscape in which we live today.

God uses wilderness to teach us to live in dependence on him. If you have so much money that you don't need to trust God for your future, give it away. If you have enough possessions that you don't feel like you're dependent on God, get rid of some of them. Don't let your assets keep you from God. Following him into the wilderness means trusting him to provide. Part of the miracle of manna is learning about God's faithfulness. Day after day, week after week, for forty years God provided "What is it?" to his people. Month after month, God led his people through the wilderness. He is just as faithful to you today. Are you willing to trust him? Are you willing to follow?

For Reflection and Discussion

1. How has God provided for your physical needs? Have you ever had to totally trust God for these needs? What happened?

2. Has God ever sent you guidance from an unexpected source? Tell the story.

3. How has your life been like a wilderness? How has it not?

9

The Battle Is Not Over

Bible Basis: Exodus 17

> Your right hand, O LORD, glorious in power—
> your right hand, O LORD, shattered the enemy. (Exod. 15:6)

A preacher described his daily battle between his old selfish nature and life in the Spirit like a fight between two dogs, a dirty brown one and a bright white one. The two dogs were equally big and equally strong as each day dawned, and they were locked in a constant battle. Someone shouted from the congregation, "Which dog is going to win?" The preacher simply replied, "Whichever one I feed."

The Israelites' journey to the Promised Land was not quick or easy. As they followed God's lead through the wilderness, they, too, faced daily battles—against enemy peoples, against the elements of the desert, and against their own weaknesses of spirit. The story of the journey from slavery to freedom is about the Israelites' struggle and about God's enduring grace. Time and again the Israelites' selfish nature rose up and they grumbled against God, but God continued to lead the people and provide for them.

Except for the Egyptians, the Israelites didn't have any run-ins with other peoples in the early part of the journey. But the deserts around Mount Sinai were home to the nomadic Amalekites. The Bible says the Amalekites were sneaky. They came up behind the

Israelites and tried to cut off the stragglers. They attacked when the Israelites were weary. They sent raiding parties among the Israelites to steal property and take captives. Worst of all, they "did not fear God" (Deut. 25:17-19). They tempted the Israelites to give in to rebellion and disobedience of all kinds.

In our journey of faith, we, too, can fall prey to enemy powers that lie in wait to distract, deceive, and destroy us. We are in battle against the powers of sin, death, and hell that want to destroy our connection with God. This is a spiritual battle where the enemy is mostly invisible. How can we fight against the unseen spiritual powers? Let's take a look at how the Israelites fought against the Amalekites.

The battle took place at Rephidim, not long after God had miraculously provided water for the people (see Exodus 17:8-16). The Bible frequently uses water to symbolize the presence of God's Spirit (see, for example, John 7:38-39). In our own lives, baptism helps us make this intimate connection between water and the presence of the Spirit. We need to understand that we fight best when the Spirit of God has filled us and is working in us. It's dangerous to fight our battles when we're spiritually dehydrated!

Moses led the battle with the Amalekites from a distance. After sending in his second in command, Joshua, Moses climbed a hill overlooking the battlefield and raised his staff toward the battle. The staff that held back the sea is again used to show God's greatness demonstrated through Moses. When Moses raised his staff, he lifted up his own identity and power, but more importantly he lifted up the greatness of God. Moses couldn't do this alone, however. He needed Aaron and Hur—his older brother and a younger man—to stand with him and help him lift up his staff.

We can't win our battles alone, either—though that's what the powers of evil would have us think in order to control us. We fall for their trap when we think that the things that enslave us are too shameful to admit to others, so we choose to face them on our own,

or when we fear what our friends, our church, and our family would do if they knew the truth about our struggles with sin, so we hold it all inside and try to hold our lives together by ourselves. We dare not give in to Satan's lie that we can make it on our own. The truth is, like Moses, we need people to stand with us and help us lift up our staffs. We need people we can trust to go with us into battle against the forces that seek to separate us from God and from the glorious freedom God offers to us. The truth is that we can trust God's Spirit to move on the battlefields of our lives to save us over and over again!

The Israelites fought against the Amalekites with every ounce of energy they had. But later, after they left Kadesh, the Israelites encountered some distant relatives—the Edomites—and they handled that situation very differently. The Edomites were descendants of Esau, the oldest son of Isaac and twin brother to Jacob. Genesis 25 spells out the rivalry between Jacob (or Israel) and Esau (or Edom) that ended in Esau selling his birthright to Jacob just to satisfy his hunger with a bowl of lentil stew and some bread! Because of this, Edom is seen as a symbol for self-centered physical desire.

The shortest route to the Promised Land went straight through the land of Edom. Moses, in good faith, asked permission to use the road and even promised to pay for any water the people might drink along the way. But Edom said, "You shall not pass through, or we will come out with sword against you" (Num. 20:18). When Israel met the Edomites on the road, what do you suppose happened? Instead of fighting, the Israelites turned aside and went around the land of Edom (see Numbers 20).

Why didn't the Israelites stay and fight? Play with the symbolism here. If, as was indicated earlier, Edom represents our self-centered appetites—our will to "gratify the desires of the flesh" (Gal. 5:16)—a different tactic is needed to wage these battles successfully. "Live by the Spirit, and do not gratify the desires of the flesh," Paul says (Gal. 5:16). When it comes to battling the "desires of the flesh," the

way of the Spirit isn't to have us wage war between our spiritual and physical selves but to learn to exercise restraint over our unhealthy appetites. The way of the Spirit is self-control. In fact, self-control is included among the gifts the Spirit gives us to live freely in Christ (see Gal. 5:22-23).

God gives us physical desires, including desires for nourishment and affection, for a reason: to enable life and to enhance the quality of our life with others. These desires are part of being human, and we can experience these desires with greater appreciation in our new life in Christ. God does not mean for our spiritual and physical natures to be at war. Rather, God's intention is for our spiritual and physical natures alike to be in obedience to his Spirit. Practicing spiritual disciplines, including fasting and tithing, can help us to grow in obedience.

Fasting is a spiritual discipline that teaches physical restraint. Giving up food—a legitimate physical need—for a short time helps us take our eyes off ourselves and focus on God. While I never enjoy fasting, I do value the spiritual strength that comes after the fact. (While I'm fasting I'm usually just crabby.) Fasting teaches me that I do not need to obey every physical impulse I experience. I can practice self-control. And fasting doesn't have to be limited to food. We can abstain for a while from any number of things to help deepen our walk with God. Declaring a fast from television or online social networks or something else that takes up a lot of our time presents opportunity to spend more time in prayer.

Tithing is a spiritual discipline of generosity. Giving one tenth of my income back to God is a physical practice that breaks my spiritual bondage to money and material things. Every time I write a tithe check, God loosens the hold materialism has on me. It's also important that I give to God first, for then I am encouraged to trust God to help me live on the remainder of my income. Doing so keeps me focused on what I *need*, not what I *want*. And when I am not

held captive by my material desires, I am better able to see the needs of others around me.

There are many other spiritual disciplines—worship, prayer, service, studying the Bible, to name a few—that help us grow stronger spiritually. The truth is that because of the reality of sin we will not be able to control our sinful nature completely. However, we can choose to feed those desires that God intends for our good. We can also feed the God-given desires of our new spiritual nature: a desire to honor God, a desire to grow close to him, a desire to tell others about him.

How do we win battles against sin, death, and the power of the devil? We do so by knowing that we have been chosen by God; by lifting up God's greatness; by lifting up his provision; by lifting up his faithfulness. We gain strength from lifting up the stories of God's deliverance in the past and, with the help of others, from lifting up our staffs—our identities as children of the Almighty God. As we lift up God's greatness, his Spirit will come to rule over our lives more and more. Whatever the powers we battle, we can trust that God will be with us and God will be victorious.

For Reflection and Discussion

1. Have you ever tried fasting? If so, what happened?

2. What do you think of the practice of tithing—giving 10 percent of your income to God? Have you ever tried it? If so, what happened?

3. What is one conflict—internal or external—that you face right now?

4. Who can you lean on when you are in a battle? Do you have at least two people who will help you "lift up your staff"?

10

Living in Relationships

Bible Basis: Exodus 18

> Jethro, Moses' father-in-law, came into the wilderness where Moses was encamped at the mountain of God, bringing Moses' sons and wife to him. (Exod. 18:5)

Before Moses confronted Pharaoh he sent his wife and children back to his in-laws. In order to be an effective leader, Moses had to be ready to listen to God at a moment's notice. Standing on the brink of the Red Sea, Moses couldn't have the distraction of worrying about his family's needs, or even about their safety. So he wisely sent Zipporah and the kids back to her father's house. But this was a *temporary* arrangement. When Moses and the Israelites were out of reach of the Egyptian military, the family was reunited.

The Bible gives us a tantalizing amount of detail about this touching reunion. According to the Exodus account, Moses greeted his family, honored his father-in-law, and invited them into his tent to eat, to tell stories, to get reacquainted. What a different picture of Moses—the man who confronted Pharaoh and led the people through the Red Sea—sitting on a cushion in his tent with his sons snuggling on his lap, feeding them bits of manna cakes and telling God-stories with his wife and father-in-law! But here we see precisely that Moses, like you and me, was a human being who needed relationships. It was okay to have his wife and children gone while

he grappled with Pharaoh, but once that job was done, it was time to come back together.

Too often, people think they have to choose between the call of God and the obligations of family or other relationships. We may think God calls us away to live an ascetic life, complete with visions, dreams, prophetic voices, and amazing revelations. God will use these tools occasionally, but more often, God works through the mundane details of messy kitchens, holiday celebrations, arguments about time management, and taking out the garbage. God is at work through the people in our lives who hold us accountable and love us as we are. Biblical spirituality does not isolate us from others; it pulls us deeper into relationships with one another—with God at the center. "[L]et the peace of Christ rule in your hearts. . . . And whatever you do, in word or deed, do everything in the name of the Lord Jesus, giving thanks to God the Father through him" admonishes the writer of Colossians (see Col. 3:12-17). Does your relationship with God honor your marriage, your parenting, your relationship with your parents, or your friendships? If knowing God and being obedient to him is at the very core of your being, he will call you back into those relationships. He may transform those relationships. God wants to be a higher priority than any human relationship, and that may cause tension. But God will not alienate you from those people.

Mary was part of a Bible study group we hosted in our house many years ago. She grew up in a family that was anything but Christian. When Mary came to know Jesus, her family laughed at her. She toyed with the idea of skipping Christmas with her family—she knew it would be a hard holiday, because for her, Christmas had come to be about Jesus, not about the presents. She prayed about it and felt certain God wanted her at her family's Christmas party. So she went. And it *was* hard. She had to endure her family's laughter when on Christmas Eve she suggested they read the story of Jesus' birth, and when she got up early on Christmas morning to go to

worship, they made fun of her again. By mid-afternoon on Christmas Day, she was exhausted. Our family was throwing a "birthday party for Jesus" that evening for our Bible study group from church, and Mary arrived just after the party started. As she walked in the door, she closed her eyes and smiled. "It feels so good," she said, "to be with people who understand." Mary knew she needed to honor her family. But she also knew she needed relationships that strengthened and supported her faith. That's why the community of believers we call the church is so important! God works through relationships with people, calling us into the "one body and one Spirit" to "lead a life worthy of the calling to which [we] have been called, with all humility and gentleness, with patience, bearing with one another in love, making every effort to maintain the unity of the Spirit in the bond of peace" (Eph. 4:1-4).

Faith doesn't just transform our family relationships; it can transform our work relationships, too. One bad habit that holds many of us in bondage is the temptation to do everything on our own. We believe it's easier to do it ourselves than to train someone else. After his family reunion, Moses got up the next morning to go to work. Jethro tagged along to watch. Like so many of us, Moses was trying to be a spiritual Lone Ranger, taking on all the work and making all the decisions for the people. Jethro was wise enough to know that what Moses was doing was not good! "You will surely wear yourself out. . . . For the task is too heavy for you; you cannot do it alone," warned Jethro (Exod. 18:18). Moses needed to ask for help. He needed to recruit and equip and delegate. Fortunately, instead of trying to do everything himself, Moses took Jethro's good advice and spread out the load of leadership. Moses' work relationships changed dramatically after that. Instead of spending his time caring for people, Moses now spent a lot of time training other leaders and keeping them on track. At first it was *more* work for Moses, not less! But in a short time, the amount of work being done was multiplied, the people were better cared for, and Moses had time to breathe. We

need to take a lesson from Moses. When we fall into the "I can do it all" trap, we miss out on God's plan to build strong relationships in our work life. I'm not against hard work—but too often, we miss God's blessings in the form of other people who can help us!

God has not called you to live or work alone. Instead, God calls you to freedom within the obligations of human relationships. Where does God's freedom lead us? God's Spirit will almost always lead us back into our human relationships—back into our marriages, back to our children, our parents, our jobs, our churches, and our communities. He longs to work through these relationships. What are your significant personal and work relationships? If the people closest to you share your faith, that is a huge blessing. They can be like Jethro giving Moses good advice from a godly perspective. If your family members are believers, they can help you glorify God even in the middle of your most intimate relationships. What a gift!

But even if you feel alone in your family, God has not called you to cut yourself off from them—unless you are concerned about your safety. They may alienate you, and there may come a time to temporarily withdraw or change those relationships. But it's also possible that God is calling you to be a witness of his goodness in a place where people don't know him. In your life at home, at work, or at school, a quiet faith often speaks loudly. (It's never about being pushy or holier-than-thou!) Your faith—even if it's just lived, not spoken—can have a huge impact over time. Spend time in prayer. Make sure your relationship with God is at the core. Then figure out how God is leading you into those relationships with other people.

When we have met God, we come back changed. And through our newfound freedom, God works to set others free. Freedom doesn't mean letting go of our commitments. God's Spirit transforms our hearts and our lives and sends us back into those relationships. God sets us free so that we can live as his followers in our marriages,

families, jobs, and communities. As we live in freedom within those relationships, we become the agents of God's transforming love!

For Reflection and Discussion

1. Think about your relationships with the people closest to you. Which of these individuals (if any) help you follow Jesus more closely? Which of these individuals (if any) present a challenge to following Jesus?

2. Do you think there is ever a time when retreating from a relationship with someone can be beneficial to your journey of faith? Explain your answer.

3. Why is it so easy for Christians to fall into the Lone Ranger role? What is hard about getting out of this trap?

4. What is one relationship in your life that needs prayer right now?

11

Meeting God

Bible Basis: Exodus 19

"You have seen what I did to the Egyptians, and how I bore you on eagles' wings and brought you to myself." (Exod. 19:4)

When we hear the story of the Exodus, too often we mistake God's purposes. God's main goal was not to set the Israelites free. It was not to defeat Pharaoh. It wasn't even to bring the Israelites into the Promised Land. God's purpose was to bring the people *to himself.* That was his priority all along. Think about the image God uses here: "I bore you on eagles' wings" (Exod. 19:4). Can you imagine what it would be like to fly on the back of an eagle? Can you imagine the terrifying wonder of it? A few years ago on a lake in the Boundary Waters, I watched an eagle fly three feet above the water like an arrow, never rising or falling for a full mile, wingtips barely touching the surface of the calm lake with each stroke. As the eagle approached the end of the lake at breakneck speed, I wondered what would happen, for it made no sign of pulling up. Then at the very last second, the eagle pulled into a vertical climb and landed softly in the top of a tall tree. The strength of the eagle's wings allowed it to do this.

God told the Israelites that he brought them out of Egypt "on eagles' wings." The Lord showed incredible strength and a graceful mastery in bringing the people out against the will of Pharaoh, the

earth's most powerful king! The eagle imagery is strong, agile—and wild. Bird experts will tell you that eagles are not easily tamed, and handling them is risky business. We ought to note that God is not tame either, and any attempt to "handle" him is *very* risky business. Hebrews records, "It is a fearful thing to fall into the hands of the living God" (Heb. 10:31). Notice that this is a New Testament quotation, not an Old Testament one. We might be tempted to think that this "fear of God" stuff is strictly Old Testament theology. But it's not!

God came to the Israelites at Mount Sinai in fire and smoke. He came in the storm and the earthquake, and they were terrified. When Moses went up to speak with God, the people had no idea what would happen to him. As he disappeared into the cloud of smoke, they had to wonder if they'd ever see him again. But Moses trusted God enough to go.

Can we trust a God like this? There is a constant temptation to try to tame God, to put him in a box and make him accessible and manageable. We desire to control what God has to say to us and when and how he acts in our lives. We don't want to have to discern God's will; it's a lot easier when the answers to life's questions are direct and concrete. Unfortunately, that isn't often the case! Even when Moses came down from the mountain, he didn't have all the answers. God doesn't promise to make things easy for us. But he does offer to be there in the midst of our questions and our struggles. God calls us into a personal relationship of faith with him: "I am the LORD *your* God, who brought *you* . . . out of the house of slavery" (Exod. 20:2, emphasis added).

Can we trust God even though he is wild, untamable, and risky? As C. S. Lewis pointed out, God is certainly not safe, but he is good.[1] This is one reason Jesus' coming was so important. Jesus revealed God's heart. In him we see God's goodness. Jesus is the visible expression of the invisible God (see Col. 1:15), and in the face and hands and words of Jesus we see God's character revealed. He's wild and untamable, far beyond us—but he's good.

Faith doesn't always make sense from the outside. I talked recently to a wonderful family from the suburbs with a nice home, nice car, nice kids, and a nice life who felt God calling them to move to Central Asia, to one of those countries that ends in "-istan." They believed God was calling them to go and be Christian missionaries in a country where Christianity is illegal. From the outside, this doesn't make sense. But they know God's character. They know they can trust in God's goodness.

The people of Israel were a little less trusting. When Moses failed to come down from the mountain, the Israelites turned to Aaron, the second-in-command, crying out for a god they could see, a god who was safe, a god created in their own image. Aaron gave in to their desires for security and made them a golden calf. If the Israelites had been a little wiser and a little more trusting and a lot more patient, they might have waited for God to act. Like Moses on the mountain, they might have spent some time in prayer. They might have dedicated themselves to listening for God's voice, or fasting, or caring for the needs of the community. Instead, they demanded divine help. *Right now.* Aaron and the rest of the Israelites should have known better. Moses had recited the covenant for them, and they had committed themselves to doing everything God commanded. Then Moses went back up the mountain to get the stone tablets from God so the people would have a permanent record of God's expectations and promises. They should have known better, but they got scared. And Aaron caved.

We have a terrible tendency to leap before we look—or more accurately, to leap before we listen. Our lives are so filled with activity that it seems wrong to be still and wait on God. Once in a while, we would be wise to declare an "activity fast." We need to make quiet spaces in our lives so that we can learn, in the stillness, to hear the voice of God. Shut off the television, unplug the computer, and turn off the iPod. Let God speak. Skip soccer practice. Take a vacation and stay home. See what God says. If you don't try to invent God in

your own image, you won't have to spend a lot of time and energy letting go of your ideas in order to embrace God's vision for your life when he finally makes his will clear. The point is that we all too quickly settle for a safe golden calf instead of the living God. God is not a tame entity we can manipulate by our prayers, our offerings, our sacrifices, our theology. God is wild and untamable, dwelling in thunder and smoke. The God who has saved us is beyond our control, and this is as it must be. God is beyond our understanding, beyond our boxes, even beyond our religious habits and dogmas.

Remember where God brought the Israelites when he led them out of Egypt? God brought them *to himself.* Not to Sinai, not to the Promised Land, not to the desert—but to himself. The fulfillment of God's desire for the people of Israel was that they be in relationship with him. God wants the same for us. He *is* present in our lives, no matter the issues, habits, addictions, or relationships that have kept us from the fulfillment of God's desires for us. God longs to free you and me from that which enslaves us and to bring us to himself on eagles' wings.

For Reflection and Discussion

1. Do you believe that God is "dangerous, frightening, and risky"? Why or why not?

2. Who is one person you would trust with your life?

3. Why is it so tempting to put God in a box? Have you ever fallen victim to this temptation? What happened?

4. Why is it so hard to wait for God to act?

12

Living in Obedience

Bible Basis: Exodus 20–21

"I am the LORD your God, who brought you out of the land of Egypt, out of the house slavery; you shall have no other gods before me." (Exod. 20:2-3)

People who don't know the Bible well often have the idea that the Bible is a rule book. Along with this perspective comes a picture of God as the Rule Maker. It's like the world is a big game board, and God has arbitrarily set up the rules for the game the way he likes them. Certain actions are off-limits just because that's the way God has set things up. Break the rules and God sends you right back to "Start" or maybe directly to "Jail"—without passing "Go" and picking up your $200.

What if that's not the way it is? What if the laws God has laid out aren't about control? What if they are more about protecting us from the consequences of our actions? We know that if we walk off the top of a building, we're going to fall. That's the consequence of our action, based on the law of gravity. Nobody gets angry with God for the law of gravity. So what happens if we look at murder, adultery, and stealing in the same way? There are personal consequences woven into all our actions. When you steal something, you really are robbing yourself. An extra-marital affair can end up destroying you and your family as surely as if you walked off a tall building. If

you spend all your time coveting your neighbor's stuff, you can be blinded to the blessings you already have in your life. God didn't give the law to set up some artificial boundaries. God gave the law to protect us.

When Moses came down the mountain with the Ten Commandments in his hands, he brought with him words written in stone that said very little about control and punishment and a lot about relationships. Through the law, God was continuing his covenant with the people. The first few commandments focus on our relationship with God. The remainder help us to have good boundaries in our relationships with other people. God wants us to enjoy life. Because he created us, he knows that we will enjoy life to the fullest when we live within certain limits. He does not give us the law so that we won't have any fun. On the contrary, he gives it to us to teach us how to live in fullness and joy! We need to understand God's heart in giving these guidelines. Picture a group of children playing football in the front yard. The first ritual of the game is setting up the boundaries. The sidewalk is one sideline; the driveway is the other. Your end zone starts at the big spruce tree, and ours is the far end of the lawn. That bump in the yard is the fifty-yard line. Have you ever tried playing football—or life—with no boundaries? You can try it, but you'll spend most of your time being miserable.

The first line in the commandments is critical: "I am the LORD your God." How do you hear that? Do you hear God on a power trip? Do you hear him ready to "lay down the law"? Try hearing that line in a different way. Try hearing God say, "I'm yours. I'm totally committed to you." Sometimes when I'm out in public with my daughters, someone will ask me, "Are these your girls?" My response is usually, "No, you've got it backwards. I belong to them." In a very real sense, my children own me. The rules I make and the way I discipline them is driven by the fact that I love them, that they own my heart. In a similar way, God has committed himself to be *your* God. He loves you with his whole heart. He gives rules and disciplines

you because he's crazy about you and can't stand to see you floundering and without a sense of his purpose and direction for your life. God wants you to know joy in him!

Think again about the law of gravity. What happens when you break this law? You get hurt. And probably about the time you're loaded into the car and headed for the emergency room, you think, "That was dumb. I'll never do that again." We go through a similar process, I hope, when we break the Ten Commandments. We damage ourselves, and then we repent. We turn back to God and say, "I messed up." Martin Luther said that the law's function is to drive us to God's mercy.[1]

Recorded in Exodus immediately following the text of the Ten Commandments is the Covenant Code. In this list of ordinances are a bunch of instructions about keeping slaves. You'd think that God would have forbidden the Israelites from keeping slaves after all they had been through in Egypt. But instead, God gave some very clear guidelines for keeping a fellow Israelite as a slave who entered servitude in payment for debts. First among the rules was that the slave was to be released after six years (see Exod. 21:2). That presents an intriguing possibility: What if the slave didn't want to go free? What if the slave loved his master and wanted to remain with him? (See Exodus 21:5.) Then God outlined the possibility of being a slave for life: "[H]is master shall bring him before God. He shall be brought to the door or the doorpost; and his master shall pierce his ear with an awl; and he shall serve him for life" (Exod. 21:6).

Why would God even allow this possibility? God wrote these laws for our benefit. We need to understand that our personal freedom is not the goal. The goal of the law is establishing strong relationships—with God and with other people. Obedience to the law is not a bad thing. On the contrary, there is amazing joy in obedience. Submission to God means that you are free from every other ruler and authority. The servant who chose to be bound to the master for life was guaranteed security in the relationship. A person

who has come to know God and has experienced the joy of serving him will not want to be set free from that relationship. Instead, he or she will say, "I love my master, and I don't want to be released. I want to serve him for life."

For Reflection and Discussion

1. Which of the Ten Commandments do you have the easiest time keeping? Which is the hardest? Why?

2. How do you react to the idea of choosing a life of slavery?

3. Look up and read Romans 1:1; Galatians 1:10; Titus 1:1; and Ephesians 3:7. Paul frequently described himself as a servant or slave or even prisoner of Jesus Christ and his Gospel. Why do you think this identity was so important to Paul?

4. What are your feelings on obedience? What ambitions or desires do you have that stand in the way of obeying God?

13

Living in Kadesh

Bible Basis: Numbers 20

"But your little ones, who you said would become booty, I will bring in, and they shall know the land that you have despised. But as for you, your dead bodies shall fall in this wilderness. And your children shall be shepherds in the wilderness for forty years, and shall suffer for your faithlessness, until the last of your dead bodies lies in the wilderness." (Num. 14:31-33)

Bowhunting for deer has always been a passion of mine. I'm excited every fall as deer season approaches. I'm a pretty good shot—at least when I'm shooting at targets. I can hit an eight-inch circle consistently from forty yards away. But I've never killed a deer with my bow, though I try every fall. I'm well over forty years old, and that goal is still as far from me as it's ever been. For years I've made excuses—a branch got in the way, I was unlucky, it was a muscle spasm, I was looking at the wrong sight pin, or the wind shifted. Recently, I missed a gimme shot at a mule deer buck in the North Dakota badlands. He was twenty-one yards away in clear terrain, standing still, and my arrow sailed right over his back! It forced me to think seriously—just what *was* my problem?

That was a big step for me. It suddenly went from being "unlucky" to being "my problem." Driving back home from the bad-lands, my younger brother and I had a good talk. He helped me see

that it's the excitement and mental pressure that I put on myself that makes me do stupid things. The longer I hunt unsuccessfully, the more pressure I put on myself. I can hit a target just fine. The truth is, buck fever is my problem. I get so wound up I can't shoot straight, can't think straight, and I fail to make the critical shot.

So now that I'm correctly diagnosed, I should be able to correct this problem. With a couple of quick therapy sessions or change in my shooting style, I should have venison in the freezer within a week, right? Wrong. Buck fever is tricky. It takes retraining my mind. When I put the sights on a deer, I need to get focused instead of going wild. Somehow I have to undo the panic and instill calmness. That's going to take a while.

I find it interesting that one word in the Bible that we translate as "sin" is an archery term. It means, "missing the bull's-eye." Just as I have an armload of excuses for missing my hunting shots, I've got lots of reasons why I disobey God and miss God's bull's-eye. I've spent my whole life getting good at certain sins. I'm like an old horse who knows the way to the barn. I plod along into sin time and time again. I am stuck in old habits.

Traditionally, we have associated the Christian life with "being good." But we're not. Yet we teach children that Jesus wants them to be good. We teach teenagers that God wants them to make good decisions about sex and drugs. We flog ourselves inwardly because we feel like we are not good enough. Or, worse yet, we congratulate ourselves because we are "pretty good" people. All of this reduces God's incredible love to a simple question of sin management. If I can minimize my sin and maximize my goodness, God will be pleased with me.

But Jesus said, "I have come to call not the righteous but sinners to repentance" (Luke 5:32), and "The Son of Man came to seek out and to save the lost" (Luke 19:10). Jesus has nothing to do with good people; he came for those who are sinful, broken, lost, missing the bull's-eye. Jesus came for *sinners*. This is why we call Jesus' coming

"good news." Telling people to be good is not good news. Every religion and every moral system has been doing that from the beginning of time. Telling people to be good is *bad* news, precisely because we can't be good! Jesus is good news because when we *can't* be good, he loves us, forgives us, and works in our lives. We don't have to be good enough to get to Jesus. Jesus has already come to us.

When God brought the Israelites out of Egypt through the Red Sea, they became heirs of his promise. When he brought them to Mount Sinai, he made his covenant with them and they became his people. Their identity was secure. But they still grumbled. They got sick of manna. They rebelled against God. That's why the Israelites lived in Kadesh for almost forty years. Those who were entrenched in the values and hierarchies of Egypt had to die. A new generation had to be raised collecting manna, trusting God to provide water, and believing that Moses would lead them into good places. They needed to learn they were wilderness people, not Egyptian slaves.

If you feel caught between God's promise and the fulfillment, you're not alone. The greatest saints down through the ages have lived in this tension, too. Much of me longs for Egypt. I long to live in a system where I'm safe and secure, where the risks and the tragedies happen to someone else. That part of me needs to die, and I need to learn to live in the wilderness with God. As much as I'd like to live in the Promised Land right now, I'm not ready for it. I need to live in Kadesh for a while.

The Lord's Prayer is written for people who are stuck in Kadesh. I think this is what it means to pray, "Thy kingdom come. Thy will be done on earth as it is in heaven." I'm praying against myself, really. I'm praying that God would not let me cling to my own kingdom, but that he would build his kingdom in my heart. I'm praying that God's will, not my will, would be done on the patch of earth where I'm standing at the moment. I'm praying that God would bring the courage and compassion of heaven and make it a reality in my life

now. In the meantime, I pray, "Give us this day our daily bread." I need God's provision, his word, his daily manna to keep me going while this rebellious generation in me dies away and I am made new into the likeness of Jesus Christ.

We will not live in Kadesh forever. Our fumbling, fearful knowledge of Jesus will give way to his fullness. Our prejudice and our pride will give way to his perfection. God has not designed us to live in the desert. We are designed for the Promised Land. But the slaveries of our past have created old ways of thinking, acting, and living that need to die. So while God does his work in us, we seek him and wait. When he's ready, he'll bring us into the Promised Land. When we were claimed by Jesus at the cross, his victory was a done deal. He conquered our sin once and for all. But we have not fully grown into the reality of Jesus' victory over sin, death, and hell. And so we walk this journey of faith.

If you're feeling stuck—like you've been to the cross, but you're not living a life filled with the joy and peace of God's promise—don't give up. Keep seeking God's face. It's very possible that you're just mired down in Kadesh, struggling while part of you dies and part of you is brought to new life. God's promises are firm, but sometimes they take time. For the Israelites they took forty years. Don't be afraid to ask God to show you how you're growing. Don't be afraid to ask others who know Jesus and who know you, "Are there places in my life where you see God at work?" Others may see you much more clearly than you see yourself. You may be focused on how far it is to the Promised Land, but they will tell you how far you've come from Egypt. In the meantime, don't be afraid to experience the joy God offers. Living in Kadesh doesn't have to be drudgery. You can learn to laugh at yourself and to enjoy the fact that God is keeping his promises in his own time. Don't worry. He's faithful. He'll come through.

For Reflection and Discussion

1. Has God ever made you wait for a promise to be fulfilled? What happened?

2. Do you agree that telling people to "be good" contradicts the good news of Jesus? Why or why not?

3. What is one part of your life you hope will be different when God is finished with you?

14

The View from Mount Nebo

Bible Basis: Deuteronomy 34

The LORD said to him, "This is the land of which I swore to Abraham, to Isaac, and to Jacob, saying, 'I will give it to your descendants'; I have let you to see it with your eyes, but you shall not cross over there." (Deut. 34:4)

Moses didn't get to enter the Promised Land. It hardly seems fair. In spite of all that he went through, all the amazing ways he obeyed God, all he put up with from the Israelites, Moses didn't get to enter the land.

Rebellion carries consequences. When Moses disobeyed God at Meribah—God had told him to speak to the rock, and instead Moses struck the rock with his staff and then claimed credit for the miracle of water—God told him he would not be allowed to enter the Promised Land (see Num. 20:7-13). Because of his disobedience, Moses lost out on his opportunity to cross the Jordan and enter the land that was promised to Abraham, Isaac, and Jacob. In one sense it is a disappointing end to the story of Moses' life.

But there is another way to read this part of the story. Every one of us lives this side of death in partial fulfillment of God's promises. None of us gets to see the completion of God's kingdom in this life. It is possible to read this story of Moses' death and be amazed at God's grace to his friend, Moses. You see, Moses got to look at

the Promised Land. God took him up Mount Nebo, just east of the Jordan River, and showed Moses the fulfillment of the promise from a distance. God graciously showed Moses the whole land so Moses could see that his work over the past forty years had not been in vain. What a gift!

What about us? What is the Promised Land God longs for us to enter? It is a fascinating fact that both in Jewish circles and within Christianity the Exodus story lives on "not as ancient history but as *our history*, as *our* story."[1] As we read through the story of the Exodus, we find ourselves wondering, Where is God leading us? What is the Promised Land? Let's take a look.

God's Presence Is with Us

As we saw earlier, God's priority in bringing the Israelites out of Egypt was to bring them to himself (Exod. 19:4). From the beginning of time, God's desire has been to live among his people. The Israelites encamped in a circle around the tabernacle, the "tent of meeting" where God was present. One translation of the Gospel of John describes the incarnation, Jesus' coming to us as God in human form, by saying, "the Word (Christ) became flesh (human, incarnate) and tabernacled (fixed his tent of flesh, lived awhile) among us" (John 1:14, Amplified). God promises that at the end of time he will make all creation new, and then he says, "See, the home of God is among mortals. He will dwell with them; they will be his peoples and God himself will be with them" (Rev. 21:3). A huge part of God's fulfillment of that promise is that we will know the immediacy of God's presence. Our partial knowledge of God will give way to the glory of seeing him face to face.

Our slavery to sin blinds us and keeps us from seeing God. We are separated from his presence. We are also separated from his insight and his perspective. Like the Israelites enslaved in Egypt, we can see only the mud of our slavery. This is why one of the most precious names for Jesus is Emmanuel, which means, "God with

us" (Matt. 1:23). One of the benefits of God being present with us is that we gain perspective. Moses climbed Mount Nebo to stand in God's presence and see the Promised Land. When God tears down the walls that close us in, he builds a platform that allows us to see things as they really are. God's presence allows us, finally, to see clearly. At the foot of the cross, we see reality as it truly is. God's covenant with us starts and ends with the promise of his presence.

Surrounded by God's People

God called the Israelites to live as a community. They were not just a collection of individuals but also one whole community rooted and growing in the reality of God's presence. We are created for relationships. The God who called the Israelites into community also calls us to live together in communion with him and with one another. And this kind of relationship is demonstrated through several qualities.

The first quality is *care*. When God is present, God's people learn to care about each other. They consistently and generously use their resources to provide for others. They feed the hungry and reach out to those in need. They give each other their time, their skills, and their assets. When one member of the community needs to move to a new apartment, another loans a trailer. When someone needs help remodeling, another shares his carpentry skills. Members of the community realize that they are not each "one" individually, but that the entire group is "one."

A second distinctive quality in this community is *fellowship*— the kind of fellowship demonstrated not by a simple "how are you" greeting but by being a real presence in the life of another person. There is a drought in many parts of western culture today. It is not a lack of water, but a lack of connection with other humans. We spend too much time in front of television and computer screens and too little time looking into the faces of other human beings. Our mobile culture means that many of us live far from aunts and uncles, parents

and grandparents. Who can you call when there's trouble in the middle of the night? What relationships have you cultivated that are deep enough that someone will come alongside you in a crisis?

The third distinctive quality of the community is *worship*. By worship, I mean more than an hour set aside on Sunday to run through the liturgy. This kind of worship includes a deep connection to God *and* a deep connection to our neighbors. God calls us together in prayer—praying for each other and praying for the world and praying for the mission God has laid in front of this group. We pray together in response to what happens day by day. We go from praying *for* each other to praying *with* each other. We recognize that we gather in the presence of a wild, good God whose presence changes everything.

Called to Freedom

The Israelites dreamed of the Promised Land as a place flowing with milk and honey. It *was* a land of plenty, but that plenty still required the Israelites to work. Once they settled the land of Canaan, they became farmers, shepherds, and traders. But God's call went beyond just holding a job. Their work—and ours—is part of God's design to bless the world. Like Abraham, we are "blessed to be a blessing" (see Genesis 12). God called the Israelites, and calls us, to build strong families and vibrant communities. We are called to care for our neighbors. We are called to be good stewards of all that God has given us. As stewards we are called to manage our own resources, to tend creation, to stand up for the least of our neighbors. God's covenant promises include a powerful call on each one of us!

What is life in the Promised Land? It is perfect freedom. Yet this freedom is a paradox because the only way to find perfect freedom is to be totally enslaved. This is precisely what Jesus was talking about when he said, "[T]hose who want to save their life will lose it,

and those who lose their life for my sake will save it" (Luke 9:24). Want to know what freedom looks like? Look at Jesus' example. The night before he died, the night before he carried the sins of the whole world to the cross, Jesus took a basin and a towel and did the chore of the lowest slave: he washed the feet of his disciples (see John 13). John's gospel tells us that Jesus did this precisely because he knew who he was and how much authority and power he had.

It is only when we know who we are in God's sight that we can give ourselves away. This "losing your life" is not a matter of weakness. Jesus' example shows us that this self-abandonment requires tremendous strength. Are you strong enough to let go of yourself? Are you strong enough to cling to Jesus as he calls you to serve your neighbor? As you cling to him, you begin to know perfect freedom in this life. This freedom will be fulfilled only after death, but make no mistake—it starts here.

What does perfect freedom look like? It is perfect submission to God's will without barriers. It is perfect service for his kingdom without fear. It is perfect sharing among his people without shame.

Perfect freedom is not just freedom from the addictions and enslavements of this world; it is freedom for wholehearted devotion to God's kingdom and his agenda. As we live in the community of God's people, centered in his presence and with his call upon us, we are set free to serve one another. Like Abraham, we are called, chosen, and blessed in order to be a blessing. Freedom means being open to receiving God's love, which immediately flows beyond us into our neighbor. Love is the character and personality of God that flows through all these things from top to bottom. If you want to know what freedom is, look at the life of Jesus. He possessed everything—quite literally—and gave it up for our sake. This is freedom. This is love. This is the face of God.

For Reflection and Discussion

1. Do you think it was unfair that Moses didn't get to enter the Promised Land? Why or why not?

2. What difference does it make to have unlimited access to God? What difference would it make for God to have unlimited access to you?

3. What did you learn about freedom in this chapter? Does this challenge the way you have usually thought about freedom? Explain.

4. What happens next for you? What specific plans do you have for how you can continue to grow into the freedom God wants for you?

Notes

Introduction

1. *Lutheran Book of Worship* (Minneapolis: Augsburg Publishing House, 1978), 56.

Chapter 2

1. "Holy Baptism," *Evangelical Lutheran Worship* (Minneapolis: Augsburg Fortress, 2006), 229.

Chapter 3

1. Did it work? Historians disagree about when the Exodus might have happened. One intriguing possibility concerns an unusual ruler in the eighteenth dynasty of Egyptian kings. He came to power as Amenhotep IV in about 1353 B.C., though he was not supposed to become king. His older brother Thutmose died an untimely death. Amenhotep came to power in his place, but in the early years of his reign Amenhotep changed his name to Akhenaten, a name designed to glorify Aten, the god of the sun. As Akhenaten reigned, he made greater and greater claims for this one god—first that the sun-god was the only god worthy of worship, then that he was the only true god, and finally that the sun was just a symbol of a truly universal God. Akhenaten had other gods' temples altered to scrub out the names of the traditional Egyptian gods. He commanded that all through the land of Egypt people worship only the one true God, Aten. Akhenaten even wrote a "Hymn to Aten" that is very similar to the Bible's Psalm 104. Is it possible that young Amenhotep—later Akhenaten—saw the hardening of his father's heart, experienced the plagues, and learned from the events of the Exodus that there was only one true God? It is an intriguing possibility, at least. Akhenaten's reforms did not last long, though. The pharaoh who succeeded Akhenaten, along with the traditional

Egyptian priests who were still around, ordered that all Akhenaten's reforms be reversed, that the temples go back to the traditional gods, and that Akhenaten's name be stricken from the lists of the pharaohs. No one even knew Akhenaten had existed until a few hundred years ago. While we can't know for certain, it is intriguing to think that maybe, just maybe, God's plan was effective and, for a generation at least, the Egyptians really did come to know the Lord!

Chapter 4

1. *Evangelical Lutheran Worship* (Minneapolis: Augsburg Fortress, 2006), 1162

Chapter 11

1. Lewis, C. S. *The Chronicles of Narnia.* (New York: Harper Collins, 2001), 146.

Chapter 12

1. See, for example, Martin Luther's *Smalcald Articles,* Part 3, Articles 2 and 3.

Chapter 14

1. Stephen Bouman and Ralston Deffenbaugh, *They Are Us: Lutherans and Immigration* (Minneapolis: Augsburg Fortress, 2009), 11.

For Further Reading

Crabb, Larry. *Inside Out*. Colorado Springs: NavPress, 1988.

Connor, Nicole. *The Journey to Freedom*. Rowville, Victoria, Australia: Connor Ministries, Inc., 2004.

Driver-Bishop, Robert. *People of Purpose: 40 Life Lessons from the New Testament*. Minneapolis: Augsburg Fortress, 2005.

Eldredge, Jon. *Wild At Heart*. Nashville: Thomas Nelson, 2001.

Moore, Beth. *Breaking Free*. Nashville: B&H Publishing, 2000.

Omartian, Stormie. *Lord, I Want to be Whole*. Nashville: Thomas Nelson, 2000.

Ortberg, John. *The Life You've Always Wanted*. Grand Rapids, Mich.: Zondervan, 1997.

Ruge-Jones, Philip. *The Word of the Cross in a World of Glory*. Minneapolis: Augsburg Fortress, 2008.

LaVergne, TN USA
20 September 2009
158389LV00002B/3/P